*"It is said that before entering the sea
a river trembles with fear.*

*She looks back at the path she has travelled,
from the peaks of the mountains,
the long winding road crossing forests and villages.*

*And in front of her,
she sees an ocean so vast,
that to enter
there seems nothing more than to disappear forever.*

*But there is no other way.
The river cannot go back.
Nobody can go back.
To go back is impossible in existence.*

*The river needs to take the risk
of entering the ocean,
because only then will fear disappear,
because that's where the river will know
it's not about disappearing into the ocean,
but of becoming the ocean."*

—Gibran Khalil Gibran, Poet, Writer and Artist

When was the last time you have nurtured the inner child in you, and listened with compassion to what it is telling you? When was the last time you have asked yourself how you really feel and who you truly are? When was the last time you stopped judging yourself, people and the way your journey of life has turned up to be and surrendered with acceptance, hope and courage?

Those questions were present in my life. Through loss, grief and fear I kept asking myself what the little girl in me would do, mostly how can I regain back her strength, courage and her ability to speak from the heart and let that be her guidance forward. In this book, we will be witnessing true stories of faith, fear, love and light and how each story, with its differences and similarities, may reflect on your own unique story of life and allow you to stop and think of yours. Forty lessons have shaped my journey within the heart and towards courage to date and allowed me to find answers to some of the persisting questions I have faced in life.

Under each stepping stone,* there is a dedicated section for you to "reflect and relate". It is your time while reading the book to stop, pause, think, reflect on each story and question, and write down your own thoughts and emotions. Under this section as well, I have added some practical tips that would help you in your journey through personal experience. Make use of this section for your

---

* "stepping stone"
Noun
An action or event that helps one to make progress towards a specified goal.
In this book you will find that not all my stepping stones in the journey were raised ones. Some of them were big rocks that I stumbled upon. Others were "resting stones" during the walk of life, and some just served as "stop stations". But all of them were necessary events and stages in my life that helped me to progress in the *Courageous Journey within the Heart and How to Live Fearlessly.*

own personal journey and express your thoughts from the heart. It is your safe space to unleash the curious and courageous little child in you. Let it be your venue to express who you truly are with love.

Do we have enough faith to trust in God's plan? Do we have the courage to speak from the heart? Can we move forward from loss and grief? Do we have the courage to love and be loved? Can we let the light within us guide us forward? Let us find out together.

My journey may differ from your journey, but we all are heading to the same final destination, and we all at the end want the same thing: To be accepted as who we are, and have the courage to be.

TESTIMONIALS

"I met Rana at one of my wellness retreats back in 2017 and was instantly struck by her positivity and charismatic personality.

Rana is a ray of light, having lived through tough challenges as a modern, intellectual woman in the Middle East, her ability to turn every situation into a positive scenario alongside compassion and respect for others is what makes her so special.

Rana's new book is a reflection of her quest towards breaking taboos in our society, empowering others and equality through love and education. A must read.

Keep rising, Rana!"

Hugo M. Mensch
Founder of Helios Retreats

"There are few people that come across you in life that can leave a spark of influence and can never be forgotten. Rana Abu Samaha is one of them. If there's one thing that I can tell you to expect from her book just as you can expect to experience when you meet her is energy, faith, humor, adventure and persistence. Rana floats like a butterfly from one place to another, sharing her positivity and child-like nature of curiosity to people all around her. She constantly seeks to improve her surroundings, her people and her relationship with the Almighty. I am truly honored to call her a lifetime friend and can't wait to see more books published in the future!"

Omar Al Busaidy,
Author of Just Read It

"Rana has seen the truth and can be a coach to all those who seek healing and authenticity."

Mostafa Salameh
Explorer, Fundraiser, Author & Motivational Speaker

"Rana, this book is a genuine reflection of you, while reading it, I was imagining you talking and telling your story. I've known you for the last five years approximately, which, as per the book, was the toughest period in your life; however, I never imagined that behind this successful, strong, confident, happy and bubbly person, you were having personal challenges and suffering. Sharing your journey is courageous; it's inspiring to see how you were able to acknowledge, accept and then change your reality and turn everything that was negative into a learning. Throughout your journey, you had a big impact on people around you, your positivity and colorful happy vibe is contagious even when you are living in a different country and not physically around.

I always imagine you with a big smile and a rainbow around you."

Eliane

"I met Rana in 2017 and her kindness, positivity and charisma were very present. It is part of who she is. If you are looking for positive energy, faith, persistence and gratitude, Rana is the right example to follow, and her book would give you all of that. A must read!"

Ziad Al Halabi
Friend and Colleague.

TABLE OF CONTENTS

1

FAITH – THE FOUNDATION

"Whoever builds his faith exclusively on demonstrative proofs and deductive arguments, builds a faith on which it is impossible to rely. For he is affected by the negativities of constant objections. Certainty (Al-Yaqin) does not derive from the evidences of the mind but pours out from the depths of the heart."

—*Ibn Arabi, Muslim Scholar, Mystic, Poet and Philosopher*

Stepping Stone One: Unquestioning Belief

"And HE is with you wherever you are."

—*A verse from the Quran 57:4 (Surah Al-Hadid)*

Story one: Whether it is my upbringing, my education at school, or my never-ending curiosity about the universe or why we are here, I never doubt God – the creator of the universe. Not everybody has this similar conviction, as we all have different definitions of the creator, and different religious and spiritual beliefs. But I always have that unquestioning belief that He is with me at all times protecting me, guiding me, loving me and that His plan is the right plan for my life. That trust has always been there; it is just the intensity of the feeling – of that conviction – that changes with time, age, circumstances and how connected I feel with myself. The more I am connected with Him, the more I am connected with myself, and vice versa.

He has been with me from the beginning. From the moment my fragile being came into this world. I was what you would call a miracle baby. Born at the end of the second trimester, I was kept alive only by an oxygen machine. I weighed a little more than 1 kilogram, and my mother said I looked like a little chicken.

I was born in Jordan, an Arab country in the Middle East and the home of the ancient city of Petra, one of the new Seven Wonders of the World; but soon after my birth, my mother had to travel back to Saudi Arabia to be with my father, leaving me in an incubator for three months. We were connected only by a phone, which doctors held against my tiny ear so that my mother could talk to me and I could hear her voice. She used to call me every day, a couple of times a day. That is how we connected during the first months. Later, she would tell me that I ended up being talkative; she claims this is because of all those early conversations. Those conversations wired my brain from my first days to appreciate the power of connection, to have a voice and share it, especially at critical times. It can save lives, as it saved mine.

The doctor told her: "There is nothing else that we, or you can do. She is in God's hands." He was right. I was in His hands, and my beloved God pulled me through and supported my being from the beginning of my life's journey.

At the age of five, He saved me a second time. A pan of boiling water flipped from my mother's stove and drenched me, scalding my entire face, some parts of my body and my back. My parents panicked; they rolled me in a blanket and rushed me to the hospital. Once again, I was in doctors' hands and in His. For a year following the burn, I saw doctors on and off to help rid me of my scars. As any child at that age, I used to dread going to those early morning appointments every day as the process of peeling the scars off my face and body was very painful, and I would come back home with a fresh sheet of special bandage covering my entire face and body. Our home was filled with mirrors, and I still remember it like it was yesterday how I used to run to my bedroom so to avoid seeing my wrapped face reflection in the mirrors. One morning, I woke up and decided to look at myself in the mirror. To my surprise, I was not scared of me, and somehow managed to look beyond the scars and just laughed at my reflection. From that day, I stopped running to my bedroom to avoid me, and decided to have an everyday conversation with the mirror, even with the scars. It was my little secret adventure at that time, and I have kept that practice of mirror's talking to date. Now after all these years, a small tiny scar is the only reminder I have on my chest. I have not always thought this way, but now I see it as a mark of who I am and where I have come from. It sits close to my heart, and when I touch it, I am reminded of the adventurous side in me and of strength, hope and resilience. I am reminded that beauty comes in different forms; what matters is what we hold in our hearts and not the scars we have outside or within. The scars shape who we are beautifully and are a part of us. I kept it and had no cosmetic surgeries done since it is a reminder of my journey and that experience of it.

Because of this and many more things, I believe everything in my life is happening for a reason and is perfectly planned by Him. Even at times when life is not turning out the way I planned and I am not understanding the reasons, I still have that unquestioning belief. It is the foundation that has guided me through life's journey.

I have always wondered if human beings can live and survive without grounding beliefs. I have realised that, perhaps unconsciously, we all have a core belief that shapes our lives and accompanies us every step of the way, with every move, without us even being aware of it. Although my unquestioning belief was and still has been my guidance, my compass, I have still lived in fear; I have been doubtful at times and broken. I have hated my life at one point and hit rock bottom.

I recognise that I had courage as a baby and as a young girl. To almost have life snatched away from me twice and then survive has been a powerful realisation. I believe we are all born with courage, but that life's stresses and pressures mean we can gradually lose it, by force or choice, and sometimes without even noticing. At times, we lose courage to please others and at other times to camouflage the pain deep inside our hearts. We pretend to be a version of ourselves that is far from the truth, and so deserted from the heart.

My quest has been to peel back the layers of who I have become and find the fearless little girl I once was – the little girl who survived against all the odds, had *heart to heart* conversations with herself, and whose life has been guided and shaped by God, who saved it every single time to date.

My first learning: We all have a belief or some sort of conviction that grounds us and gives us the strength and courage to live life fearlessly and lead from the heart. That would be your compass and grounding thought. Everything else in your life will evolve around it, even if you have not been aware of it at some point.

Reflect and relate: Think of at least one of your grounding beliefs that has shaped your life. It is crucial in your life to identify your belief system, so you can break through from the limiting ones that are blocking your journey.

Below are some common examples of misbeliefs. Do any of them sound familiar?

- I am not strong enough;
- I do not have enough time;
- I am too old, or too young now to change my life;
- I have to stay in this relationship because it is difficult to find another;
- People do not change. I cannot change;
- I am responsible for people's happiness;
- I will be happy only when I …
- I cannot …

_____

_____

_____

_____

_____

Stepping Stone Two: Trusting the Inner Voice

"There is a voice inside of you that whispers all day long,
I feel this is right for me, I know that this is wrong.
No teacher, preacher, parent, friend or wise man can decide
What's right for you – just listen to the voice that speaks
inside."

— *Shel Silverstein, Writer*

Story two: When I look back at my life, I am continually struck by that image of me as a little girl. I had a unique identity. I was restless too. I was always told I move too much, and my mother keeps telling me and her grandchildren up until now how sorry she felt for me that I had to sit for such long hours at school when I was young – a torture for such a hyperactive and restless child.

I was a perfectionist too. Every morning, I used to get up and dress up like a little doll, always making sure I had matching socks and shoes. For me, dressing up was – and still until now – not only an avenue for expression, an expression of identity, but also a reflection of my inner deepest emotions. I did not know it then, but perfectionism would become a curse rather than a blessing when I became an adult – a way of controlling my happiness and contributing to the opposite.

Nevertheless, as a little girl, I was experimenting, never fearful of what others would think or say about me. I would speak up, confident in my opinion, and confident about who I was in my head and in my heart. At a certain age in my childhood, I was a tomboy, maybe because I sensed that my father would have, deep down, wanted to have a son. I remember that most of my childhood neighbours were boys, and I was part of the boys' squad as the goalkeeper in an all-boys' football team. I nailed and earned that position in my neighbourhood. I used to jump triumphantly after blocking that brilliant shoot from entering as a goal, leaping to save the ball and tumbling to the ground. I still remember all the bruises I used to return home with at the end of a day after playing football in the neighbourhood streets, and the look in my mother's eyes. But I was good at it, and I felt free and liberated. The two contradictory sides of me have been very obvious from my childhood days. The yin and yang. The softness and the toughness. I trusted and experimented with both sides as they reflected my inner self at that time.

Academically, I was a high achiever. Even though I am a Muslim, I attended Rosary Sisters School – one of the leading Christian schools in Jordan – for my primary schooling years. This is very normal in Jordan. We all live, study, work and unite in harmony, regardless of our religion, ethnicity and background. That is what I have always admired about this country. The sense of belonging that all of us feel. I have always believed from a young age that God is for all and He is for everyone and anyone. That feeling of acceptance of others and the illusion that we are different was a thought that has always been with me and I have sought to explore it more. Schooling years were the best years of my life. The school was nearby and I used to protest every morning to my parents that I want to walk to school and not be driven by my father. Some days, I used to win this argument and found myself tossing in bed the night before from excitement. Walking to school with a heavy backpack full of books would not be so appealing to others, but for me at that time, it was refreshing and adventurous to walk alone like a grown up looking at the outside world from my own lens. First thing I used to look at was the sky and count how many shaped clouds I could see until I reached school, which was a journey between five and seven minutes depending on my speed, and the detours I took to follow the candy man in the streets selling our all-time candy in the eighties: "Pink Cotton Candy." I developed the practice of walking at that young age, and have kept it since. Today I can walk sometimes up to twenty kilometres a day without noticing. I have all the time admired wandering and observing the outside world and everything in it from nature, architecture and human beings. Walking has always served as my time to think, destress and rejuvenate my soul.

When I moved to high school, I aced it. During that period of my life, I was inquisitive and crazy, romantic and stubborn. I still remember falling in love (or what I thought so at that time) when I was a teenager and I was convinced that I would get married at the age of eighteen in the name of love. My sister made fun of me, and she still does – about how romantic and unrealistic I can be at some times, but I kept challenging her that this is who I am. The core of my being. Now with my boys being teenagers, I can see some of those traits in them, especially the stubbornness in my youngest son and the continuous protestation and persistence if he believes in something and wants it badly. I chose to live life on my own terms as a young adult within the parameters of what was religiously and socially acceptable at that time. But I did try and ensure, most of the times, that my parents, especially my father –may his soul rest in peace – were supportive of any decision I wanted to make in terms of planning my future and my studies abroad. Yet, I truly believed in my intuition at that time and listened to my inner voice, even if I did not know exactly what to make out of them. But, I kept listening to them and playing with their tunes. I lived a life that was carefree, happy and exciting, knowing somehow that I was in this world for a reason. That was what my inner voice would always whisper to me.

My father – may his soul rest in peace – would tell me: "Just be happy. Live in the moment." What wise words any father can say to his daughter. I used to nod not fully comprehending what living in the moment meant, or how to make myself happy. But the sound of his words was very pleasant for my ears to keep hearing, and I kept repeating his words and even using them in my arguments with him: "But you have told me to be happy and live in the moment. I am just following your advice!" I used to tell him smartly. I did not know back then that those words of him would become the main lyrics of my inner melody that I have kept chanting in my journey of life.

As I grew older I slowly lost the little girl in me. I forgot how to be passionate and curious like her. At times, I lost my inner voice telling me who I was and how to be just happy. I could not hear those whispers anymore and unintentionally blocked any melodies within. Where did that person go? What happened to that child? Later, after experiencing different kinds of loss and grief I was determined to search for that little girl once again. Life and loss can harden people's hearts, but I vowed that never to happen to me. Somehow, it softened me and I was able to search deep inside and found that inner voice telling me that this was my story, my journey. I cannot change it, even though others may choose to judge me. Through darkness, I have learned to take ownership of my life and trust myself. Trust in those "nudges of truth," as I like to call them that I get often when I am tuned in, aligned and centred. Gaining the confidence back in trusting my inner voice and repeating my father's words as my mantra were not easy tasks, especially when I thought that it has betrayed me and led me to an undesired direction. I lost trust in it. I lost trust in my ability to take the right decisions anymore. But it was not my inner voice that betrayed me; it was the other way around. I stabbed it in the cord, and let it bleed till silence! With my foundation of unquestioning belief and giving room for my inner child to emerge back to the surface armed with my trust in Him I have been able to open the channels of communication within me. To align the inner voice with the outside one, until they both speak the same language. They both reflect the true me. I kept looking deep within myself, learning to listen gently to my inner voice and gaining the little girl's trust in her own intuition until I became more steadfast in trusting my intuition as a grown-up.

My second learning: Listen to your inner voice. If you lose your path in life, then it should be about the journey to undertake, and how to hear those whispers of truth back again. Have faith that your inner voice will eventually guide you on that journey, and never lose hope that it will be your faithful companion throughout.

Reflect and relate: Do you trust your intuition? If you would allow your inner child to speak to you now, what would it tell you?

> Inner voice can have different names. It can be referred to as "intuition," "inner guide," "spiritual guide," "inner wisdom" or whatever you choose to call it. The question is, do you trust it?

_____

_____

_____

_____

_____

_____

_____

_____

_____

_____

Stepping Stone Three: The Dark Side of Questioning Everything

"We can easily forgive a child who is afraid of the dark; the real tragedy of life is when men are afraid of the light."

—*Plato, Greek Philosopher*

Story three: Even with my unquestioning belief that grounds me, there have been times over the past decade when I have questioned everything. How could I hold on to my belief in Him when the world turned against me? How could I understand the universal plan when my life fell apart? How could I pick up the shattered pieces of my existence having only my faith in God as my guidance? How could I do that when the silent anger that I felt burned me to my bones, leaving me shapeless – just a flame burning inside and out? When my father passed away in 2014, it was as if my soul had been ripped from my body, leaving it as a hollow shell. My father understood me. He knew I was different, and he loved me unconditionally. Throughout my life, he had been my rock, the one person who never stopped me from being me and fulfilling my potential. He used to call me "the volcano", knowing me well that I always turn my life upside down. When I went to the UK to study law, he was my biggest supporter. He knew the traditional path followed by most women in my culture was not for me.

In 2010, and only after one month when I moved to Abu Dhabi, the capital of the United Arab Emirates, he was diagnosed with cancer. I still remember when he called me to tell me that he had already finished his operation and that he had cancer in his thyroid. He assured me that he was doing great in health and spirit and I should not worry. I was in the hypermarket getting ready to pay and everyone could hear me yelling hysterically: "What operation! How did you operate without telling me! How could you all do this to me? I am coming back now." I left the shopping trolley without paying and managed to crawl out from the busy mall with my young boys at that time, telling myself that nothing would be the same after this day. I was right, nothing was the same anymore! I could not travel back to Jordan immediately, as at the same time my marriage was falling apart, and I had to stay to give it one last chance.

My father had been admitted to different hospitals, and undergone all possible kind of treatments including the painful journey of chemotherapy. I could not be there with him all the time as I was in Abu Dhabi dealing with my own internal issues at home alone and making sure his health was the priority. I could not see him heartbroken from my sadness and misery while he was already encountering the last painful battle of his life. For the coming years ahead, me and him were both fighting our different battles of life, but his was the last. Seeing his grace, courage, positivity and love of life during it all made me stronger and gave me guidance in dealing with my own.

I had met my ex-husband eight years earlier while training to become an admitted lawyer to the bar in Jordan. I loved his sweet words at the beginning, and I saw in him a person whom I could be with and have a family. By the time my father had been fighting his last months with cancer, my ex-husband had decided to return to Jordan alone and our two beautiful sons were with him as it was clear that we could not continue with this marriage any longer, for the benefit of all of us, but mostly our sons. The pain of not seeing them, even temporarily, was unbearable. On the day I filed for a divorce, I opened my door to an empty house – a house that had once been filled by my children's images and voices.

I remember lying in the darkness that night consumed with all sorts of grief and pettiness. Hours passed as I prayed, digging so deep to understand why this was happening. "I will always have faith in You, and You will take me through this," I kept praying to God. At the same time, I felt so confused. Was this His plan for me? For my family? For my sons? I told myself that if I got through this endless night, if I did not die of a broken heart and awoke the next morning, then nothing could break me.

I did wake up and found strength that I did not comprehend for the months ahead. Just as I will never forget the anguish of that night, I will never forget the sight of my father's life slipping away shortly after my divorce. He was always such a talkative man, such a kind and loving person. Now, as he lay in the hospital in Jordan, words eluded him. He could not speak, and I knew in my heart that it was just a matter of time before I saw him and held him for the last time.

For months, he had paid for my airfare to see my sons and to travel home back and forth every weekend from the UAE; he used to support me in any kind or manner and always got my back. I still remember, on the last day before he died, just before he lost consciousness, he slipped a letter into my pocket, along-side some money and a note: "Rana 'Habibti,*' please take this money for the last ticket." He could not speak in his last days

---

* "Habibti" is an Arabic word that is commonly used to show affection and love. It means darling or my love in English.

before he passed away, he was frail and hooked by the machines, yet he managed somehow to write me that note with perfect pronunciation and beautiful handwriting, as a farewell note. A reminder of how eloquent and selfless he had always been, and that he would still take care of me until the last breath, literally. As I read it over and over, I sobbed uncontrollably. I knew that it was time to let him go, as he had protected me all those years. Now I know he is all around me, protecting me still, in the same way God has always done. His last farewell note forced me to question everything including why he had gone too soon because I was not ready to say goodbye, and I had no idea what to do without him. Yet his last farewell note was a hidden message for me to keep following his trail in kindness and selflessness through my own journey.

My third learning: Questioning and doubting are natural phases in our life. At times it will be difficult to see the light through the blinding pain. Be kind to yourself. Know it is part of the journey. Embrace it even if you cannot understand it. It will pass.

Reflect and relate: Write down an experience that forced you to question many of your beliefs in life and how you dealt with it.

> Remember that questioning means considering all options that would lead you to better understand yourself and what next steps you want to embark in life.

_____

_____

_____

_____

_____

_____

_____

_____

_____

_____

Stepping Stone Four: Patience

*"And be patient [O Muhammad], for the decision of your
Lord, for indeed, you are in Our eyes."*

—*A verse from the Quran 52:48 (Surah At-Tur)*

Story four: I have always been impatient. Being that bright and curious child, no sooner had I accomplished one task, than I was on to the next. No breaks in between. No time to waste, and no patience to endure. Even now, I am a whirlwind. I talk quickly and I act quickly.

I remember being at school and thinking I understood everything, so why did I have to study all these years? Is there a short cut? How can I finish earlier and go to the next level? I felt the same when I went to university to study law; I got my degree within three and a half years, ahead of so many of my peers, yet the years seemed so long. Same when I came to the UK to complete my masters. I wanted to graduate within a year and start working immediately, which I did. I was never good before in pausing, slowing down, reflecting deeply and just waiting. I have always felt there is something or someone waiting for me to upgrade to the next level. That person was me. I have always been in a race with myself from that day when I was so eager to come to life three months earlier.

Through years, my patience became stronger, and God kept giving me the strength to endure and be patient, even at times when I felt I was sacrificing parts of my life and giving to others a big chunk of me, if not all. Yet when my sons were born, I had to demonstrate patience to them as a parent. Our children want to be seen and heard especially at younger age. They are like a sponge absorbing the outside world, and I wanted them to see and feel at earlier age that in me as a parent. My eldest son was a colic baby when he was born; that meant nonstop crying for hours especially at night. I was twenty-eight years old when he was born, and had no experience handling babies as a new mother. I used to stay up all night with him trying to figure out what was wrong with him. While he was crying, I was crying too. No one can prepare you for motherhood. You cannot take a class or course on it; you are just thrown into it and learn from experience. I used to stay up all night with him until early morning. He used to sleep while listening to the birds' dawn chorus. That used to soothe him, and it still until now soothes me too. My day would have just started and I had to prepare myself for work. I have always been a working mother, as I need to keep stimulating my mind and intellect. I get bored easily and need new challenges and environments to keep me on my toes. So early in my career, I had to learn gradually and train myself to take extra time, be patient, follow thoroughly the logical process and adapt to the business environment that expected me to persevere, endure and tolerate.

When my marriage began to disintegrate, I experienced patience in its fullness. I wanted my relationship to work. I wanted my children to get a glimpse of the love of a stable family. I did not rush into taking decisions; on the contrary, I delayed, procrastinated and endured.

The truth is, I had many chances to leave. Instead, I chose to stay longer than I should have. Apart from being patient in taking such a critical decision, I believe I had also gotten used to living an illusion, instead of opening my eyes to reality. I was so afraid that people would judge me if I left. I was terrified that I would be seen as a failure and that I would see myself as such. Fear was holding me back. I needed to find that fearless little girl within and take a step into the unknown. It was patience that allowed me to see that, not immediately but eventually.

In thinking of this journey, I am always reminded of the song by late Whitney Houston, "I Look to You." I used to play it several times a day, pausing, repeating and singing along the part when she tells God that at times when her strength has gone, her faith in Him was strong, and eventually His light would shine upon and within. I, too, have felt exhausted by life, lost as to what direction to take at some point; but somehow, I have found my route, and patience was the key to open the doors of hope: the doors of change. Now, I can see parts of my life as if they were all part of a bigger puzzle; every piece of it contributes to the overall picture. I can see the transformation behind the sorrow and pain of my father's death, as well as the joy and satisfaction of his life when he was alive. I can truly know what love is when I think of my sons, and I can also know why I endured so many years of unhappiness with a partner.

When I look at this now, I understand that patience is a gift that allowed me to go through this process. It allowed me to see who I was, who I had become, who I wanted to be and how I could begin the long road back to happiness. Every time in my life, when I am close to giving up on myself, deep waves of patience hit my shores and carry me through. I see patience as my everyday blessing, propelling me forward. The more I endure, the more patience I have with myself, the people around me and the journey of life. As ironic as it sounds, after transforming myself from that little impatient girl to who I am now, I joke with my friends that "patience is my second name!" It is; and every time I whisper in my heart that verse of the Quran (52:48 Surah At-Tur) that says: "*You are in Our eyes.*" I smile with deep certainty at "Al-Yaqin" inside and endure more.

My fourth learning: It is a cliché that whatever does not kill you makes you stronger, but it truly does! When you ask for patience it will be given to you. Pray for it, it is one of the truest blessings in life to have the strength to endure.

Reflect and relate: Remember a verse, a quote, or a saying that you repeat every time when you are looking for patience inside of you.

Some tips to train yourself to be more patient:

- Figure out your triggers;
- Make yourself wait;
- Embrace those uncomfortable feelings;
- Breathe, and breathe even more;
- Keep practicing.

Stepping Stone Five: Finding Connection

*"All that is left to us by tradition is mere words.
It is up to us to find out what they mean."*

—*Ibn Arabi, Muslim Scholar, Mystic,
Poet and Philosopher*

Story five: Despite whatever happened in my life, I have always found the connection back to God. Even now, in my everyday life, I take time out to pray, meditate and talk with the universe and Him. Through this, I understand more about myself, and I feel grateful for what I have. That connection makes me grounded and liberates me at the same time. It gives me wings to fly.

For those people who are not religious or spiritual, there are many ways to find this connection. Some people refer to this as connection to the source or the universe or being present. It is the connection back to who we are, the very core of our being and an acceptance of where we have come from. Everyone's journey is different, even though we may all be going through similar challenges and struggles.

At times, when I have questioned about everything, I have been afraid of losing this connection. It has been weak, fuzzy or broken. But I have fought with every fibre of my body and soul to find it again. In 2016, when I was still grieving my father and I had to accept that my sons would not live with me, I travelled the world to find this connection again. I wanted to experience life and the universe in different forms, in new ways and in a deeper sense.

I will never forget that on the last days of one of my journeys I sat on the most magical beaches in Bali. But I did not see its beauty. Instead, tears ran down my cheeks and turmoil tormented my mind and body.

For the whole time I had been on the island, I had been searching. "Please show me a sign. I know You love me," I kept repeating to God. But when you are searching so hard for a sign, it never comes. Yet, on that last day, it did come. There, resting in a black thunder cloud was a heart-shaped cloud peeking out amid the emerging light, perfectly formed and showing me the way.

From that moment on everything changed. My connection was restored and I began my journey back to me. Having that hope has kept me waking up each morning with the same passion and enthusiasm as I did when I was a little girl.

Now, when the days are tough I know how to reconnect with my true self and ask the little girl in me: "How is she, really?" With my grounding belief, the restored connection with Him, and my daily practices of prayers and my Dua'a – the prayers of request, which are the very essence of worship and connection from my perspective, my faith deepens and I listen within myself to the messages I tend to receive and to the signs I am meant to see. The people I meet, the decisions I make and the situations I find myself in are all part of His life's plan for me, even if I do not understand why at times – even if it took me a decade to understand why my life unfolded the way it had.

In fact, after the toughest of times, I know that this connection is not lost, rather it has deepened and strengthened.

Now I see that connection everywhere. When I walk in the park near my home, I visit my favourite tree. I notice how the crisp and golden leaves drop in autumn, and in the spring how they are renewed with life and colour. I see the connections in the clouds too. All those walks back and forth to school, when I was young chasing the clouds, allowed me now to immerse in their beauty. I see those heart shapes in their formation all the time, there for a moment, then moving and changing with the wind. These are such small pleasures in life, but each one of them anchors me.

My fifth learning: The most important connections you have in life are those with God, the creator, the universe, and within yourself. Those connections, if nurtured well, can grant you peace and tranquillity throughout.

Reflect and relate: What is your favourite practice to nurture the connection within yourself?

Some of my practices are:

Prayers;
Meditation;
Yoga; and
Walking in nature.

Stepping Stone Six: Purpose of Life

"The meaning of life is to find your gift.
The purpose of life is to give it away."

—*Pablo Picasso, Artist*

Story six: From a young age, I wanted to be a lawyer. I had watched the US TV series *Ally McBeal* about a young female lawyer working in a Boston law firm and loved it. Especially Ally used to have those mirror's conversation in the office bathroom. I thought that resembles my daily mirror's conversation that I have established since that day I looked at myself in the mirror and high-fived my scars. Of course, I saw myself as well, defending clients and making a difference in the world by serving other people. It was my dream.

When I did end up practicing law, the reality was a little different. The pressure, the stress, the demand and, because I am a woman, the perception of that continuous need to prove myself every day at work and in life. It was as if being a woman is a stigma to break. I started working in corporate law in different roles and companies, then moved into compliance roles at a later stage. I have always been good and passionate about my job and love it. It gives me the opportunity to connect with people and make a difference. It has taken me around the world which is something I love to do: meeting new people, cultures and being in different surroundings have always appealed to me. It is my sweetest spot. No wonder that I am constantly on the move.

Yet, even with success bolstering me, I was unsatisfied emotionally. I did not fully understand where I fit in life or my true place in the world. I did not know who I was or why I was here. Through the most difficult of times, I struggled to find my purpose, and to know what God's plan was for me.

As a girl I was always challenging myself, and when I think about it now, I understand that I have never stopped doing so. In my career, I have always pushed myself forward. I was never one of those people for whom life was all about going to work, going out, coming home and repeating the cycle again. I was always searching for meaning and fulfilment.

With my career and travelling, I was able to obtain luxurious material possessions and I was very thankful for that; but something was missing. I had friends around me and I lived comfortably, but I was not satisfied. Through grief and heartache, this hole kept getting deeper and darker. At times, it was as if I was drowning: my body was being dragged further down to the icy depths of an ocean floor, and I felt like gasping for breath as I plummeted further downwards.

Then I realised that although I had everything I needed, I had lost myself. I had become trapped in a place where I could see no way forward, no path to begin my journey back to happiness. I was numb: numb to my surroundings, my own emotions and numb to life itself, confined in this prison of false satisfaction.

Through faith, my purpose in life started to reveal itself gradually but deliberately. On the beach in Bali that day when the cloud revealed to me a heart, I knew my way forward. I knew I had to heal myself first. No amount of success, shopping, luxurious materials or any connection with other humans can bring me satisfaction unless I force myself to take some time to understand who I am, and what I want.

I have always thought that I am an extrovert as I am talkative, can easily start any conversation with others, and do not shy away from being in the spotlight. But the more I started to dig deep within me I discovered I am a thinking introvert. I discovered that in my late thirties! No wonder I have always craved alone time, and felt exhausted when I am surrounded by people for so long. As a thinking introvert, we are often deep in our thoughts, wondering about life and analysing ourselves. I still like social meaningful gatherings and outings, being in the spotlight, and I do not mind the presence of other people, but not all the time. As a thinking introvert I am in continuous reflection whether after reading a book, watching a movie or having a conversation with a friend. One time, I wrote an essay after watching *The Notebook* movie for a third time – it is an adaptation of the 1996 romantic novel by American novelist Nicholas Sparks, and one of my all-time favourites. I was analysing the romance and love relationship between Noah, Jr. and Allie Hamilton and reflecting on my life and relationships. I did not know back then that I had an excuse to spend hours of time comparing my relationships with those of Noah and Allie. In my defence, I would have blamed the introverted thinker in me.

I started reading more and writing, and getting to know myself and my life's purpose. I enrolled myself in different courses to grow, to discover myself and what interests me, to discover what ignites my being and why I am here. One of the courses was to become a certified life coach. Inspiration appeared all around me, like dust caught in the light.

Through the death of my father, losing my marriage and my sons being away from me, I was forced to stop and reflect on life. My purpose has always been to serve others and help whether by choosing to be a lawyer, a life coach or an author. This has always been present; this is something I am destined to do. To find a higher purpose is to have the courage to look within your heart and hear its heartbeat, without judging, wanting or expecting. To listen with love, and let it guide you to that purpose.

My sixth learning: We all have different talents to share with the universe and the people in it. Do not shy away from who you are and keep searching to find your purpose. You may find it now or in many years, as long as you give yourself the chance to listen within.

Reflect and relate: What is your purpose in life?

> Did you know that there are four types of introvert:
>
> - Social introvert
> - Thinking introvert
> - Anxious introvert
> - Restrained introvert

Stepping Stone Seven: God Is Love

> *"Beloved, let us love one another, for love is of God,*
> *and everyone who loves is born of God and knows God.*
> *He who does not love does not know God for God is love."*

—*A verse from the Bible (1 John 4:7–8)*

Story seven: What is pure love? It is a question I could never answer when I was younger. But, when I started to heal myself, I realised that I have been loved by God, which is the purest form of love, ever since my tiny fragile body entered this world. He has been with me since day one, even before.

I now know the person I am today comes from that love. Even during those times when I have lost my way, or strayed from the path, He loved me unconditionally, and kept me full and complete.

I believe that about other people, too. I believe that people are born to be good. We are all born with innocence and love in our hearts. But life changes us. People suffer traumas; they live with cruelty and violence; others live with pain, poverty or ill health. All these things can wander people away from their lives' purposes and stop them from fulfilling their potentials. All these things can lead people to forget about pure love.

It is so easy to judge other people who we feel do not live up to our own life expectations, or those who are different. I know this because I have been guilty of it. I have not been kind to others all of the time. I thought I was perfect, and I knew better – I criticised others who did not do as I did, or did not understand me the way

I wanted them to do. I was guilty of wanting people to be copy and paste versions of myself. I was guilty of thinking that my way is the only right way. I was guilty of thinking I knew it all, when in fact I know nothing at all, and I am still learning. How many of us are guilty of that!

Even back at high school, I judged my friends. I used to go in my perfect dress with perfect hair and make-up eagerly, ready to sit for the exams. They had been studying all night and morning. "But it is so easy!" I used to say to them. I was criticising them for being different, for studying longer hours and feeling stressed about exams! I could not understand how they did not think in the way I did.

Later, when I started working, I wanted things my own way: my way or the highway. I was competitive, but not in a great sense, when I think about it now. I was only thinking of myself. My own success. My own achievements. It was so often about me, and not "us." Sometimes I was even preaching to others what I did not do myself. Even at the beginning of my coaching journey I was telling others what to do and was chastising them inside of me if they did not. "You must meditate!" I can hear myself saying. Must is not a word to be used if you are enlightened and if you are leading with God's love.

I did not understand, as I do now, that everyone is different with their own ways of thinking and that we are all unique in our own existence. I could neither force people to be who I wanted them to be nor did I want to do that, I realised. Instead I could show them kindness, understanding and forgiveness. I can lead by love, and it is their choice to follow that path or take a different route.

In being kind to others, we are being kind to ourselves. We are passing on the gift of love that God has given us. Everything grows from this love: the love of Him and ourselves, the love of people around us and the love of life and all God's creations. This is because God is love, and it is the most natural emotion for all of us to feel, spread and experience.

With His love, I found "Rida" which in Arabic means true satisfaction.

My seventh learning: Once you stop questioning everything, everything opens up to you including God's love. His love allows you to be true to yourself and to help other people. It is the purest form of love.

Reflect and relate: Have you been guilty of judging others who are different from you? What can you do to start your journey of acceptance?

> Try this: think of a friend or loved one who is judgemental of others or you. Write a letter advising them to stop that and express how you feel about it. Now read that letter loudly to yourself by putting your name where their name is. How does it feel to treat yourself like you treat friends or loved ones?

Stepping Stone Eight: The Outside World Is Just a Reflection of What Is Inside

*"Your life is reflecting back to you exactly
who you are all of the time."*

—*Oprah Winfrey, Media Executive, Actress,
Talk Show Host, Television Producer and Philanthropist*

Story eight: After divorce, I came home every day to unbearable emptiness. My sons' bedrooms stayed the same as they were, but they were lifeless and dark. The joy that they had brought to my life had vanished. There was no laughter, no curious questioning of life, no enthusiasm or passion for anything.

When I looked at myself in the mirror, I looked tired and drawn. I wondered where my life had gone. The memory of the person I had been had become so much dimmer. I became consumed by fear that the memory of my two sons being with me would fade, too, like the light from the sun when it slowly sets over the horizon.

I put myself in the "victim" category for so long. All my focus was on how unfair life was, and all my energy went into that destructive idea. This was the narrative playing over and over in my head: I was alone; I was consumed with anger; I could not love or be loved. How often do we say these terrible things to ourselves and not even notice them? How many of us believe this negative inner voice telling us we cannot control our destiny, and turn our lives upside down, but this time turn to the good side of life, the lighter side?

What I did not realise is that my negativity about myself was like a magnet sucking in people and situations around me, which were bad to me. I was attracting people who did not serve me, and who would, in the end, make me feel as though I was a victim once again. I became a magnet for people to abuse my energy, emotions and time.

I could not see it then, but it was only me who could change my destiny and my reality, and break that vicious circle. But narratives cannot be changed in one, two or even three months. To vibrate higher, we need to learn how to train ourselves every day by changing the way we speak to ourselves. How we address ourselves automatically commands how others address us. It dictates the outside dialogue. Exercising that muscle that allows us to accept ourselves and look towards the light rather than darkness needs discipline.

When we are in that negative place, we blame everybody else, except ourselves. But blame is no use to anyone. It swoops and circles around like a vulture looking for its prey. I told myself it is time to take accountability of my own mistakes, learn from them and find courage inside of me to break that blame circle once and for all.

I could have turned to unhealthy habits or just lived my life with anger until it consumed me to death, with my anger weighing down on me so I could barely breathe. Instead I looked to the things in life to be grateful for, and slowly started to drink in life, tasting all the elements of the universe that were healthy rather than toxic.

I started being thankful for what I had and what I have every day. The more I am grateful, the more blessings I receive along the way in my journey.

From the moment I learned how to let go of my negative inner narrative and channel it in a constructive way, my life changed. I was not a magnet for destructive people or damaging situations anymore. Changing my focus and energy on what is positive and what I am grateful for in life changed everything around me. I figured out, it is as simple as this: We attract what we are, and the depth of our feelings and actions is a critical variable in attracting what we want in our lives. What we vibrate inside reflects in our outside world.

My eighth learning: You cannot change other people. You can only work on your inner self and change your inner narratives so you can vibrate higher and attract what you want in your life. When you start to change, everything around you changes.

Reflect and relate: What is the current narrative that keeps playing over in your head?

> Your mind is a magnet; you do not attract what you need or want, but you attract who you are at any moment of time.

_____

_____

_____

_____

_____

_____

_____

_____

_____

_____

_____

Stepping Stone Nine: I Surrender

"But perhaps you hate a thing and that it is good for you;
and perhaps you love a thing and it is bad for you.
And God knows while you know not."

—*A verse from the Quran 2:216 (Surah Al Baqarah)*

Story nine: From an early age, I mapped out my life: I would be successful at school and in my studies. I would have a glittering career and be swept off my feet by a handsome prince. After a whirlwind romance, I would marry young in a beautiful white dress and I would live happily ever after. I wanted to have a perfect life – the kind you read about in fairytales; well, who wouldn't. But what was my avenue for expression when I was younger now started to imprison me as an adult. I planned my life ten years in advance. I guess you could say I was a control freak, and it started to choke me.

After I gave birth to my two boys and they grew up, I wanted to control their lives too. I was consumed with panic when they were not dressed properly for the cold weather or when they had a high temperature. Later, I would worry if they injured themselves playing or wanted to try new adventures. I worked myself up into the state of uncontrollable panic. I did not want them to go outside or be touched by life in case they were hurt or harmed in any way.

When life is unpredictable and your dreams are left shattered by life and loss, when you are thrown into the unknown, then the urge to control everything around you intensifies further and this strategy becomes counterproductive and painful. Even in my prayers, I now admit I was a control freak, and controlling felt like a sugar rush; every time you start with a small piece, you end up wanting more. I was asking God for specific things – a good job, a nice home, a happy marriage and healthy kids. These are all justifiable prayers I would repeat, but I wanted my prayers to be answered within a timeline I planned for myself, rather than completely surrendering to His perfect timing. I have learned that this is a recipe for self-destruction. Turning all your fears inwards so it changes your expression of life and your enjoyment of it is so damaging to yourself and to the people around you.

Over time I have learned to surrender, learned to make the best out of what I have, even if it does not match up to the fairytale or to the plan in my head. Learning to be at one with my authentic self did not happen overnight; rather I learned to navigate and accept that God knew what I did not know, and the overall plan is perfect and complete.

When I emerged from questioning everything – questioning His love for me, questioning my faith and my place in this world – my sureness grew stronger. What made no sense before, suddenly became clearer. If I wanted to move forward I must learn from the past, look deep inside my soul and make changes to ensure I followed a happier path – a kinder path. I understood that stepping stones in the journey are not always consistent, raised or flowing. Sometimes we take steps back and sometimes there are steps forward. But they are all essential and leading us to our destination. Sometimes we do not realise why we are on a certain path, and this might only be revealed to us years down the line. With all of this, I have chosen finally to surrender and accept. To let go of my ego that kept poking me consistently to be in control of life.

Knowing that what you have now is the best for you and that you will emerge from darkness is a message I have repeated to myself day after day. Through it, something bigger about the world was revealed to me – something bigger than my life. My faith has led me to surrender and accept what life shows to me.

My ninth learning: Losing the urge to control everything around us is freedom. Enjoy the flow of life as it comes.

Reflect and relate: Are you a controlling type of person? Choose three things that you want to give up controlling, and start today.

Here are some signs from personal experience that you might be a controlling person:

- You want things to be predictable and stick to a routine;
- You can be demanding and critical;
- You have extremely high standards for yourself and others;
- You feel anxious when things do not go the way you want or expect.

_____

_____

_____

_____

_____

_____

_____

_____

Stepping Stone Ten: Certainty

"What you seek is seeking you."

—*Rumi, Poet, Faqih, Islamic Scholar and Sufi Mystic*

Story ten: Certainty is a state of being. It is knowing that He is with me, guiding me and loving me 100%. It is knowing that whatever life brings – good or bad – He will be there, protecting me and allowing me to learn the lessons of life for the future. It has always been destined to be part of my path.

Certainty did not come until later stages in my life and completed my faith cycle. It was neither present during the time of my marriage nor when I grieved my father as we will witness in the next chapter.

Back then I knew only the teachings of God, passed down to me through my parents and my education. I followed them blindly, not understanding or appreciating their true meaning – the reason for my very being. Throughout my life, I could have let my faith evaporate like smoke when my prayers were not answered. I could have turned my back on God, but I could not. There has always been that voice inside that kept telling me to trust the journey even when the path was not clear. Even when the path was invisible.

Reaching this higher level of certainty has allowed me to accept and embrace what life throws at me, and stop questioning the truth, rather than opening myself up to more knowledge. Trust and certainty do not mean being complacent; on the contrary, they have been my driver, my inner engine for change. I started writing down and repeating with conviction every day in the morning all prayers and mantras of trust and certainty. Feeling every word deeply in my heart. I always keep a small paper with the word "Certainty" written on it in my pocket, on my laptop, near my bed and anywhere I can see it. It has become my love word to myself and my loved ones. Our little secret and our recipe for our lives together. Certainty becomes what connects me with others, and what keeps us bonding and united.

Certainty for sure has helped me to thrive in life and not just survive and has taught me that everything is eventually going to be okay. Yet how can we thrive when fear overwhelms us, grips our hearts and stops us in our tracks? With fear as our only companion, we cannot let life in. We cannot enjoy its pleasures, notice its beauty or understand its mysteries.

Fear is still there as we will discover in the next chapter; it is the catalyst for growth but it does not overpower me anymore. It has taken me to the edge, but on the other side is a wonderful world waiting for me. It is the same wonderful world I opened my eyes to as a child and I am rediscovering it with the same passion and curiosity. It is the same wonderful world that is waiting for you as well to discover.

My tenth learning: Be certain of your journey and the connections you encounter along the way. Do whatever you can to cultivate that certainty in your heart.

Reflect and relate: Do you trust your journey so far. How can you strengthen that trust?

Last degree of Al Yaqin "Certainty" is called haqq-al-yaqin (the level of certainty gained through experience), that is certainty as supreme truth.

2

FEAR – THE CATALYST

"Fear is a negative emotion, unless you're facing an actual threat and need to fight or flee."

—*Deepak Chopra, Author*

Stepping Stone Eleven: Understanding Loss

"Because God is never cruel, there is a reason for all things. We must know the pain of loss; because if we never knew it, we would have no compassion for others, and we would become monsters of self-regard, creatures of unalloyed self-interest. The terrible pain of loss teaches humility to our prideful kind, has the power to soften uncaring hearts, to make a better person of a good one."

—Dean Koontz, Author

Story eleven: A person can live with fear well before the loss happens. I learned this from the moment my father was diagnosed with cancer. In some ways, living with the fear of loss is as terrible as the loss itself. Constant thoughts of the loss of loved ones or even their own deaths would chain a person and paralyse them from living.

Yet, I lived with the fear of loss from an early age. Perhaps it was because I was separated from my parents when I was first born that I experienced heart-stopping anxiety whenever they left me. If ever they went at night to see their friends, I would lay awake, waiting for the key to turn in the lock, calmed by the knowledge that they were home safe.

As an adult, fear gripped me in similar ways: fear of my marriage failing, fear of losing my sons and fear of my loved ones dying. Before the loss of my father, I used to believe that expressing emotions and saying I love you to people was a sign of weakness. I did not tell my father I loved him enough, and I never knew that losing him and my boys being away from me were the first steps in me opening up and talking about my feelings.

Even then, this lesson took time to be revealed. In the first two weeks after my father's death, I was silent. Frozen. I did not even cry. It was Ramadan, the Muslim month of fasting, and he had passed away on the tenth day. Instead of expressing my feelings, I broke my fast by eating chocolate to comfort my broken soul, I still remember. I became thin and lifeless. I did not nurture myself through my grief. Instead, I turned my attention to other people.

My mother, who had just lost her husband, needed comforting. Likewise, my sister needed consoling. She had been there every day at the hospital with our father. Before that, she had spent months tending to him during his sickness and watching him become smaller and frailer.

My boys, too, had lost their grandfather and I felt so bad for them. They were still trying to comprehend why I and their father were not together, and why we were not a family unit anymore. I put on the mask of strength by talking less, feeling less and being less. I was numb with the loss, as if I could not absorb it in one go.

My father's situation got suddenly deteriorated ten days only before he passed away. I still remember that day; it was first day of Ramadan, and I had a phone call from my sister at 9:00 a.m. UAE time, which was surprising: "Rana, come now to Jordan," she urged me. All I was praying on my way to the airport is for me to be able to see him and talk to him for the last time, and for God to be merciful to grant me that wish. I usually have high intuition about things, and I could sense from couple of days before that call that something would happen to our father. That is why I was crying nonstop all that week without knowing why, or actually because I knew why!

I arrived Jordan at the right time and managed to see my father in his last days at the hospital lying there helpless and in pain. It was the first time that I actually prayed for God to help him out of this misery and pain. I could not tolerate seeing him in such a condition, and was thinking that death would be better for him. He would be happier and pain-free out there. Still when the time came for his beautiful soul to return to its creator, and although the first thing I have done unconsciously is praying a thankful prayer to God that He released my father from his pain, loss was unbearable and could not be handled. It could not be explained, only felt. It could not be understood, only lived. The only way to overcome it is, unfortunately, by feeling it all fully, completely and with no holding back.

Now I know that loss of any form can take years to overcome. Instead of opening up at the beginning, I became more angry. I was scared. I was fearful of the unknown: fearful of a life without my father who guided me, fearful of how I might take a step forward. Fear stunts our forward progress and emotional growth; it blocks our interaction with our inner spirit and it generates disharmony in our relationship with God.

To overcome fear, I had to comprehend the real reasons why I am afraid and realise that my fears are pointing to the places within me that need attention. These are the places that need unconditional love and spiritual understanding, in order for me to continue to evolve, grow and overcome loss.

Nevertheless, loss has taught me to be humble, kind and compassionate. It opened my eyes to what life is truly about. In time, loss has revealed to me who and what is important, and how short life can be. Loss forced me to ask these questions daily: How do I want to live my life? Do I want to live it in agony? What legacy do I want to leave behind?

My eleventh learning: Express and let the people around you know you love them before it is too late. Loss might shake you and you will never be the same person again, but it reminds you of what matters. It reminds you of how to live life and celebrate it every day – for yourself and for people that you have lost.

Reflect and relate: If you have experienced loss in your life in any kind or form, how did that loss change you?

> "I know you are listening from above. There is nothing that I value more than your love. No matter where I am or what I am doing, your memories will always keep me smiling."

_____

_____

_____

_____

_____

_____

_____

_____

_____

_____

Stepping Stone Twelve: Overcoming Grief

> *"No one ever told me that grief felt so like fear. I am not afraid, but the sensation is like being afraid. The same fluttering in the stomach, the same restlessness, the yawning. I keep on swallowing. At other times it feels like being mildly drunk, or concussed. There is a sort of invisible blanket between the world and me. I find it hard to take in what anyone says. Or perhaps, hard to want to take it in. It is so uninteresting… I thought I could describe a state; make a map of sorrow. Sorrow, however, turns out to be not a state but a process. Grief is like a long valley, a winding valley where any bend may reveal a totally new landscape."*

—C. S. Lewis, Author

Story twelve: By the time my father passed away, I was already in grief state. I was grieving for his loss but also for the loss of my marriage and the break-up of my family. My mother wore black years before my father's passing, when he was diagnosed with cancer, as if she was preparing herself for his death, but also because her soul was already saddened by his sickness and weak state; but I did not, that is, not for so long. I continued to wear bright colours even after he passed away – he loved the reds; but inside my soul felt as black as my mother's widow's garb.

Perhaps because I did not change my dress, my outside appearance, I mastered hiding the pain and the broken side of me. People around me saw me as superhuman, even cold. They asked, "Isn't she grieving? Isn't she sad?" They judged me: "Why is she living alone abroad and not with her mother now?" All those questions and judgements that people believe they have the right to say especially at a time of grief! It is amazing how everyone becomes an expert in everything and anything when you are grieving. All I needed at that time was the space to be with myself and figure out day by day how to get through this. I was also pretending to be superhuman. I did not see my grief as any less real if I wore red or black, and if I disguised my turmoil, then no one would prick me and hurt me. The truth was that I could not let any more grief in. If I did, I thought I might collapse, or shatter into tiny pieces that I would have to pick up from the floor of my existence, unable to repair.

For more than a year I could not look at my father's pictures or visit his grave. My father was well-loved by people. In our neighbourhood I could not bear listening to people talking about him. It was too hard to accept that I would never hear his voice again or talk with him. Fear was the only emotion holding me together at that time. It was my only best friend at that time. When I look back now, there were signs that I had spent many years prior to his death living with fear. For months after he was diagnosed with cancer, I clasped my mobile phone next to me wherever I went. It would sit beside me as I slept, and if it rang or beeped I would jump and answer it that second. I was in continuous anxiety, hidden to the world. As all these panicked thoughts circled around in my head, I worked harder, sometimes eighteen hours a day, to mask the pain. Even though people close to me warned me I could not survive this lifestyle, and given the way I was camouflaging my pain I would surely break, I ignored their advice to look after myself first. I was putting off the inevitable process of dealing with the unresolved anger and anguish I was carrying around with me like a dead weight.

But in my own private time, I felt overwhelmed. The minute I shut the door to an empty house I cried. "One day you will be blind if you keep crying like this," one friend told me. I could not see it then, but those feelings would pass, and they did. I wish I have a magical wand or formula to tell you how to get through grief easier, quicker and pain-free, but the truth is it is a process we have to get through. What I learned about this process is that the more you delay dealing with your feelings transparently, and be ashamed of them, the more complicated, painful and lengthy the process would be. Within time, I learned not to hide grief, my tears or my sorrow. Somehow this allowed me to emerge as a more complete person.

Slowly I allowed myself to gaze at his pictures for a second or two even if tears rolled down my cheeks. After more than a year, I managed to pay my first visit to his grave. I went with my sister and our kids because they missed their grandfather and wanted to visit his grave. I was very nervous, and I remember that my sons at that time, even though they were five years younger than now, gave me support and told me: "You can do it, Mama. You are strong." The first experience was mixed with tears and laughter. I mentioned before in the book that I move quickly and talk quickly so I could not help it but stumble near his grave. We ended up all laughing hysterically.

I knelt closer and whispered to him: "I am glad in my first visit, I made you laugh." I could hear him replying back to me: "You are my volcano. You will turn things upside down again for sure. Keep laughing."

My twelfth learning: Grief is a process that we might experience at certain points in our lives. Take your time and be gentle with yourself. The more you delay the process, the harder it becomes. Do not judge others who do not grieve in the same way as you do.

Reflect and relate: How gentle are you with yourself when you are sad or grieving? Do you allow yourself to experience it fully?

Some amazing benefits of crying:

- It helps release stress;
- It helps your body bounce out from trauma;
- It signals to others that you might need support;
- It is cleansing and soothes physical pain;
- It allows you to be happy too.

_____

_____

_____

_____

_____

_____

_____

_____

_____

Stepping Stone Thirteen: Being in the Comfort Zone

"I am not angry. I am not sad. I have no questions. I need no answers. For, I am numb. I can't cry, I can't smile, I can't laugh, I can't giggle. For, I feel numb. I don't argue, I don't think. I don't talk, I can't fight. For, I feel numb and Somehow, I just know being 'numb' is worse than anything else!"

—Jyoti Patel, Author

Story thirteen: Not long after my father's funeral I returned to Abu Dhabi. Many family friends expected me to return home to Jordan to be with my mother, sister and my sons, but Amman was not the best place for me.

During the funeral, which lasted for three days, family and friends visited the house to pay their respects. For me, it was a difficult time. People had not seen me since my divorce, and I could hear them gossiping. "She is very beautiful; how could this happen to her?" I heard one woman said. My father had just passed away, but it was as if I was the one on show: people were coming to see the divorced daughter.

Although on the outside I appeared still, I felt suffocated. I wanted to be alone, cry my eyes out and surrender myself to grief, but I could not. Instead, I had to smile, be polite and be surrounded by people who passed judgements. So much of my culture is about what you show on the outside, but I know it is who you are on the inside that matters. I promised myself, not to attend any funeral after my father's. That whole experience made me question the way we support others at time of grief. There are so many different ways to pay respect and support the people you care about. Attending funerals was not one of them for me, I realized.

The same happened when I returned to work. I had tried so hard to hold myself together. Being an outspoken successful woman, I felt I had to carry on being so. I tried so hard so no one could see through the cracks where my heart was breaking. I handed in my resignation at work and got a job at a new company where no one knew me and I could blend in. There I could camouflage my true pain.

I had told no one that I am in a grief state when I joined my new company. I recall one day when I opened up to one colleague, I had lost so much weight and I felt zombie-like, sitting at my desk every day. "You are in this situation and you have not told anyone?" this person said, horrified. I used to think that sharing how I feel was a sign of weakness, not knowing it is totally the opposite.

My days were the same. I got up, went to work and returned to an empty house. My soul was empty. I was existing rather than living. I had no vision, no goals and no compassion for myself or those around me. No real interest in anything new. I had shut down my emotions, shut down expressing them to others just to protect myself. I was tired. I wanted less noise in my head and around me. I was living in the comfort zone for more than two years after my father's death.

So many of us live life in the comfort zone. We exist rather than live. We walk around on autopilot. At times like these, we are not conscious of people who we let into our world, of the decisions we make. We merely want the days to pass. We are numb. We do not open ourselves to experiences that nourish us, help us or bring us to a place of acceptance. It is only through a continuous search for life that we can rise up and participate in life, so it can act the same upon us.

My thirteenth learning: Thriving in life and being the best version of yourself, for you first and then for others, is rarely done in the comfort zone. Yet, your comfort zone is your "resting stop." Use this time to reflect, connect, heal, search and decide what you want in life.

Relate and reflect: Be truthful to yourself, are you living in the comfort zone? Is it serving you well? If not, what can you change?

Take this challenge to step out of your comfort zone for a minimum of five continuous days:

Day 1: Set your alarm for ten minutes earlier than usual. This is your extra ten minutes to do something different;

Day 2: Dedicate ten minutes at least every day to learn something new;

Day 3: Take a different route to work, or start your schedule differently;

Day 4: Tell someone how much they mean to you;

Day 5: Journaling using the reflect and relate section.

_____

_____

_____

_____

_____

_____

Stepping Stone Fourteen: Finding Acceptance

> *"I am my own biggest critic. Before anyone else has criticised
> me, I have already criticised myself. But for the rest of my life,
> I am going to be with me, and I don't want to spend my life
> with someone who is always critical. So, I am going to stop
> being my own critic. It's high time that I accept all the great
> things about me."*

—*C. JoyBell C., Author*

Story fourteen: If we really listen every day to the internal dialogue we have with ourselves, the stories we tell ourselves, we
would be shocked at what we could hear. It was not until I started
listening that I realised how critical I was of myself.

Just as I was on autopilot at points in my life, I was also on autopilot in my head but with a negative, nagging voice. I heaped criticism upon criticism on myself to the point where I hardly noticed
any more. These messages ranged from telling myself I was not
good enough at my job, to not being a good enough mother, a
friend, a lover and the list continued. I kept pushing myself, trying
to prove something to myself first and then maybe to the outside
world. Then, I punished myself for not being with my father every
day before he died. I criticised myself for being tired, for dreaming
big, or for wanting peace. So many times these thoughts perme-
ated my mind and I had little compassion for myself.

Instead of spending time nurturing myself, I wasted so much
energy analysing what went wrong in my life. I did not look back
to understand nor looked forward with optimism and hope. I lost

sight of the little girl I once was. I had only questions for God, for my faith and for myself but was not willing to find answers. I had only questions of judgement and resentment. I dwelled on guilt and shame instead of being curious about how I might change and why I want to change.

As these negative thoughts overwhelmed me, I took no risks in life. Doing anything different or new might have the possibility of failing, getting hurt, and I was not prepared to take that risk. I had convinced myself that the comfort zone was the safest option for me. But slowly, I started letting light back into my life by accepting. Accepting everything that happened, every piece of it so far and everything that will.

My father had passed away. Whereas before I could not let any memory of him in, now I see myself as his legacy. He was a man bursting with life, love, kindness and wisdom. If I did not live in the way that he had lived his life and brought me up, I would not be honouring his memory.

My sons are not with me, but instead of letting this affect me and worrying about every little thing they do, I learned to appreciate what we have and feel the blessings that are around us as they are plenty. I learned to step back a little. I stopped fighting and resisting the situation. I learned that resistance only ignites more pain. It fans the flames of conflict.

Instead, I started to see life through a different lens. My sons were being well looked after. I am still their mother and can give them all forms of love, support and security they need in different ways – new ways, unorthodox ways. I can talk to them when I want and tell them how much I love them. I can still nurture them, care about them and play a vital role in their upbringing even if I cannot be with them every single day. I can love them with every bone in my being. I discovered this is what kids need: love, love, love and more love. Actually, that is what all humans need: love.

As I moved to this place of acceptance, I started to make peace with whatever had happened in my life. I let the events of the past wash over me. I could not hide it any longer – this illusion that I had been living. Instead, I started to see my life clearly and more compassionately.

I remember, I was sitting in my room one night looking so deep within my tired soul. It scared me how I had let my soul slip into sadness for so long even if I was not showing this to the outside world. At that moment, something inside of me protested for the last time: ENOUGH. ACCEPT. LET GO. MOVE ON. That time I listened, agreed and promised it to take action.

This did not happen overnight. Acceptance needs practice like any virtue in life. I started building up my world and moving on with life. Little by little I started to embrace the world around me. Every day I took a step further towards the light.

My fourteenth learning: Acceptance gives you a different perspective. It allows you to accept the things you cannot change and gives you the courage to change the things you can.

Reflect and relate: What does "Acceptance" mean to you?

Tips: There are many types of meditation that can help you to accept and let go. You can start your practice with as minimum as ten minutes a day then build it up.

Stepping Stone Fifteen: Am I Good Enough?

*"Do the best you can until you know better.
Then when you know better, do better."*

—*Maya Angelou, Poet, Singer, Memoirist and Civil
Rights Activist*

Story fifteen: From the time I began the process of acceptance, the little girl I once was started to break through the surface of my despair. Before, I had been drowning, overwhelmed by sheer loss, but now as my body floated upwards it was as if the sunlight sparkled across calmer waters.

Even so, I was still weighed down by the fears of adulthood. While my younger self was saying: "Go for it," my adult mind was torn between two worlds. If I was going to see my life from a different perspective and turn it now upside down, I was going to have to dig deep to find myself. I was going to have to look in all the places where I could be exposed, and to magnify parts of my life that had been painful. I would have to put down my sword and shield of defence and fight the war with my own mind.

Most of all, I started asking myself whether I was good enough to live without pain. God knows, I had lived with it for some time. I began asking, am I good enough to be happy? Am I good enough to be loved? Am I good enough to start over again to start something new? Am I good enough to be just me?

Often our negative self-narrative tells us we do not deserve happiness, we do not deserve to be loved. We do not deserve second chances. If we let life in again, there is a possibility we can be hurt by it. Life opens up all our soft and tender parts and leaves us exposed. After living years of life without a true identity was that a risk that I could and want to take?

What I started to realise is that my feeling of not being good enough had been guiding my life so long. This was the inner dialogue that had made me work so hard, to push harder and be in constant chase of something, someone, an illusion. It had moulded me to be a people pleaser, always trying to give to others instead of making sure I was satisfied first. It had been controlling me all these years and pushing me to make poor choices in my life. If your inner dialogue does not serve you anymore, it is time for a change.

Armed with this realisation, I looked at the friendships and relationships that were not fulfilling and revaluated so many of my engagements with people and where I was spending my time, effort and energy. I distanced myself from toxic people – the emotional vampires, they are the people in our lives that sap our time and energy. These people are never there for us when we need them. It took time and practice to detach myself from those people and take my power back.

Now, I was faced with a new dilemma. What was I going to do about the path that I had now started to embark on? Could I really rebuild my life on new additional foundations? Did I have the courage to change? If life is about constant renewal, who was the person I was going to be if I changed? I was on the verge of living fearlessly and listen to my heart, but I needed that one final push to jump.

My fifteenth learning: Be persistent in finding answers. It is easy to fall back into your comfort zone, but exploring your past and your present is the way to build your new future foundations.

Reflect and relate: Write five reasons why you are good enough.

Examples why I am good enough because:

I was chosen to exist, and because I am here;
I have something that no one else has to offer;
I make big mistakes, huge ones but that is awesome because
    they give me the chance to learn;
I choose to love;
I am vulnerable.

_____

_____

_____

_____

_____

_____

_____

Stepping Stone Sixteen: Shall I Just Jump?

"Do the thing you fear to do and keep on doing it, that is the quickest and surest way ever yet discovered to conquer fear."

—Dale Carnegie, Writer and Lecturer

Story sixteen: Before last decade, I had rarely travelled alone except for my studies abroad. I had always been travelling either with my family, my ex-husband or my friends. I wanted to start exploring my life and myself through travelling alone, so I decided to become a solo traveller.

I thought of all the most beautiful places in the world I could visit, but I was still scared. I did not have a partner accompanying me. I did not have my sons to travel with. My family were far away, and my plans at that time did not match with my friends', so I kept postponing it further, worried that I would not manage alone and worried about facing the unknown in starting the adventure of travelling alone and exploring.

Even though I still had fear existing at that time, I started travelling alone for different reasons while making sure to plan for the next one before the existing trip finished. To my surprise, I became addicted to travelling. In one year, I travelled alone to Rome, Barcelona, Paris, Amsterdam, New York, Boston, the Maldives, the Seychelles and Bali, to name a few. In each and every place, I allowed myself to explore freely. I opened myself up to new experiences in ways I had never thought would be possible before.

I had always feared water, and maybe I still do to a certain extent, but in the Seychelles I snorkelled in the shallows. The fine, white sand gave way to the vivid aqua blue of the sea. Below the surface, butterfly fish parted as I swam through the coral while manta rays floated effortlessly below. Suddenly, I started to see life differently. A world with light that I had somehow dimmed was now filled with colour, in its pure form, reminding me of my love of the sea and my love for nature.

I tasted new food, talked to strangers, embraced different cultures and realised I was bringing back my real me to the surface. And I loved airports too. A perfect place to bring my thinking introvert character to the surface loud and clear while observing the constant flow of people, reflecting about all busy living life, and letting my mind and soul wander. It opened my horizons to a world that was vast and wide, not small and narrow as it had been over the last few years.

Of course, there were times when I was alone and frightened, and questioning why I am even here in foreign cities, but I kept moving, exploring, looking within and forward knowing that He is always with me. Sometimes I marched forward, other times, I barely took one step after the other, but the key was to keep moving forward, taking one step at a time. I even found the courage to return to London after all those years, the city where my first son was born, and I had so many memories that reminded me of joy, opening a new chapter with deeper understanding.

Later, when I returned to London to complete a course in motivational training, I was filled with even more courage and love to myself. As part of one conference, I chose to fire-walk to overcome my fears by walking barefoot in front of thousands of attendees across meters of burning hot coals.

Being a burn victim at a young age, I had to dig deep to find that courage and break free from that fear. I had become terrified of switching on a gas oven! As for the fire-walk I did not want to do it. My body froze as the crowd chanted and the embers glowed in front of me. "Go for it. You can do it," I kept telling myself, and the only thing I remembered is crossing to the other side with tears running down my cheeks. Tears of inner triumph. I was winning myself over and that was and still is my biggest and proudest success: to keep winning myself over.

With every step I took, I felt a newfound confidence, a light guiding me to a new way of being. I never knew how much grief and loss had affected me before that point; how I had allowed myself to shrink into a shell of feeling fearful of the world around me. The fear existed, and although I was not completely fearless, I had allowed myself to experiment with life and emerge from the shadows.

My sixteenth learning: We do not have to be completely fearless to open new doors in life, but by experimenting and pushing our boundaries we can learn to jump with less resistance.

Reflect and relate: If you can choose one thing that you want to experiment now in life, what would that be?

My coming two adventures:

Swim in the sea and skydiving

_____

_____

_____

_____

_____

_____

_____

_____

_____

_____

Stepping Stone Seventeen: Wake-Up Calls

*"In the absence of wake-up calls, many of us never
really confront the critical issues of life."*

—Stephen Covey, Author

Story seventeen: I have learned over the past few years that however much you plan in life, the outcome can become unexpected. You can prepare for all situations but sometimes events you cannot control happen. Life can feel like a roller coaster, speeding over highs and lows, while you desperately grasp the rail. When you finally get off, you are left dizzy and bewildered about how to carry on.

While some events led me to shut down to life, there were two wake-up calls that gave me the will to decide to thrive in life and not just to exist and to appreciate my being, and I now believe these were all part of my journey.

A few months after my father's funeral, I was admitted to hospital suffering with a searing pain in my back and stomach and a raging fever. Not long after I was diagnosed with gallstones. I was shocked but I should not have been surprised.

I had been living through fear and with fear. All that negative energy that had been swirling around in my mind and my body had now revealed itself. I had not nurtured myself at all – barely eating, not expressing my emotions to anyone and only letting them out in my most private, darkest moments. I had surrounded myself with toxicity, corroding any happiness I could feel.

Before the operation, I had to remain in hospital, as the doctors had ordered, but I also found that hard. The last place I wanted to be in was a hospital, any hospital. The memories of my father's death flooded back, and I did not want to be reminded of him being there, helpless and nearing the end of his life. Fear gripped me. What if I was operated on and did not wake up? What if the anaesthesia would put me to sleep forever? As it was administered by the surgeon I lay there trembling. "Please make sure I wake up," I pleaded fanatically.

I did wake up and I did survive. It was as if God was showing me what mattered in life and that I am here for a purpose. I had my health, I had my boys and I had my family. I had started seeing the beauty of the world. I had begun to learn that when you cannot control your outside world, it is the perfect opportunity to start focusing on what you can, what is inside, which is you, your thoughts, your sanity and your being.

This was tested two years later, after I had embarked on my self-discovery and spiritual journey. I again became sick, but this time the experience was entirely different. I had developed lesions in my liver, and although they turned out to be benign, I read this as another sign. Two years separated me from the panic of the anaesthesia but my reaction was totally different that time, as if I had become a completely new person. This time I had certainty, faith and knew how to heal myself alone. I trusted Him completely; therefore I trusted in the power of myself.

Instead of curling up in a tight ball of panic, I taught myself slowly but surely how to listen to my body and trust it. I said to myself the words that the doctor had told my mother all those years ago.

"There is nothing I can do. I am in God's hands." This was my mantra. With my faith in Him I prayed every day. I thanked Him for everything I had. I felt grateful for the small things in my life, but most of all I knew that whatever I have to face, I would do it with courage, grace and open arms.

My seventeenth learning: Signs are always around us; be aware of them. Pause and be still to read them and understand the messages they are telling you. Trust in your gut feelings; they always tell the truth.

Reflect and relate: What did your wake-up call(s) teach you?

My prayer: "Dear God, thank you for the abrupt wake-up call. I got it now."

_____

_____

_____

_____

_____

_____

_____

_____

_____

_____

Stepping Stone Eighteen: Finding Joy in the Moment

"I know now that we never get over great losses; we absorb them, and they carve us into different, often kinder, creatures."

—*Gail Caldwell, Writer*

Story eighteen: When you are in the grip of loss, you find little pleasures in the world around you. You rarely take a moment out to see the beauty in the clouds, in the sky, in the ocean, in the city, in your friends, family and social gatherings. Instead, you dwell on the past, turning over in your mind consistently what went wrong, and why, ruminating and chastising yourself. Or, you start worrying about the future. Never focusing and enjoying the moment.

Finding joy in the moment takes practice, pausing, awareness and just letting the moment absorb you fully. So often we let the present slip past us, like a thief stealing time. We are on our phones, laptops, work desks, reminiscing about the past or worrying about the future; we are half-focused on the world around us. We are not being mindful of our surroundings and the beauty they vibrate. We are always busy or pretend to be, as we think it is safe when we are busy, rarely able to sit quietly with ourselves to find a moment of calm: a moment of pure joy.

Yet beauty is everywhere, but it is a personal responsibility to find ways to tune into its frequency. Focusing on being rather than doing gives us the space to observe our thoughts, to know they are momentary, that they do not control us and we have the power to change them. Instead, we become a compassionate observer of them, understanding that we have the capacity to be strong and, at the same time, weak and vulnerable and dance with the contradictions of such. Our thoughts lead us to a place of empowerment. They let us rise from loss and become reborn.

After my years of travelling and exploring my inner self, I began to transform into a different person. I resolved to make the best of what I have. I told my boys, as I do now, that God has a plan for us. It is grand, even if we do not understand why we are on this path. I tell them, "Have faith and live in the moment." It hit me while I was writing this paragraph that I was actually channelling my father's words to my sons all these years and passing his wisdom back to them. The lyrics of my inner voice from him are now theirs. And I know as I am planting those lyrics in them to guide them, they would do the same with their kids and the cycle keeps on moving flawlessly.

As I started changing, so did my experience of the world. Everything seemed easier and thriving. Life became effortless, as it should have been. I had come to a realisation that pure joy does not come from outside, but from within. We can choose to find it daily because it is there and has always been around us. Once my mindset changed, my life shifted dramatically in a good way.

Today, I treasure every moment, every trip, every adventure and every moment of silence. I appreciate my walks on the beach. There by the sea, breathing in the salty air, feeling the sand between my toes, bathing in the warm water and feeling the sun on my skin. One example of free moments of pure, simple yet tremendous amount of joy. I stopped living in fear, I stopped trying to control the world around me. I stopped planning and directing life, and instead, I let life direct me. I noticed in myself a freedom, the same freedom with which I expressed myself when I was young.

I started waking up being grateful that I am being given another chance to live a new day. And when we are grateful, magic happens in our lives. Life starts becoming one moment of joy after another. I realised I have a list of dozens of things that make my heart jump, my face smile, my soul giggle and my body become energised. I call them moments of pure joy: whether it is exchanging a smile with a stranger; walking with my favourite hot coffee to work; being silly and groovy with my friends; receiving morning greetings from my boys; hugs from loved ones; watching ten episodes of *Friends*; having a fabulous conversation with a colleague at work; a moment of silence; talking to the sky; listening to one of my favourite songs; having a hot shower at the end of the day, and saying "I love you." The list is so vast and expandable by the hour that everything and anything how trivial might seem to others can actually bring joy once you fully comprehend and emerge in that experience.

Now I make a daily conscious decision to increase my moments of joy as part of my gratitude practice. It turns out to be one of those rare constructive cycles of life. You thank more, you experience more moments of joy. You experience more moments of joy, you become more grateful and the cycle keeps rolling beautifully and in harmony until it becomes seamless, shapeless and effortless, until joy and gratitude unite in one's soul.

Over that time my relationship with my sons even transformed. Children are so sensitive to the energy around them and especially to their mothers', and for many years I had tried to hide the darkness from them, shield them from the reality of our lives. But kids sense anguish. They know when something is not right, and there is something bothering me. They became happier, funnier, enjoying life and started living it with enthusiasm.

Now, I am so grateful for the moments we spend with each other. Whether it is *face-to-face* or online, we laugh a lot. My boys are so funny, smart, kind and full of love. This is the reflection they see in me now and this gets transmitted to their own beings. Every time I see them they give me more strength, resilience, joy, love and a motivation to become the best version of me every single day.

My eighteenth learning: Joy is right here. We have to widen our horizon to see it within us. Pure moments of joy are free and accessible to everyone.

Reflect and relate: Find out what brings you joy and make sure to experience those moments more during your day.

> If you can carry joy in your heart, you can heal any moment.

_____

_____

_____

_____

_____

_____

_____

_____

_____

_____

_____

Stepping Stone Nineteen: Finding Courage Within

*"There is a stubbornness about me that never can bear to
be frightened at the will of others. My courage always rises
at every attempt to intimidate me."*

—*Jane Austen, Novelist*

Story nineteen: Battles come in many forms, but it is the battle
that we face and overcome internally that truly shapes our lives.
As I arose from grief, I slowly allowed my inner child to seep back
into my being: the little girl who always knew the truth and who
always had courage.

That little girl had the strength to be different from the others
and did not care about what people thought that allowed her to be
herself. She had the courage to speak about her opinion in class.
She had the desire to love and be loved. She understood that life is
to be lived in the moment, not stuck in the past or worrying about
the future. She was fearless when it came to adventures and new
ideas. So often, we lose that inner child through the fear of society, fear of judgement and ultimately fear of us being happy and
fulfilled back again.

But, as this book shows, the journey towards courage and
within the heart does not happen overnight. Becoming comfortable with who you are and trusting in your inner voice all
take time, sometimes a lifetime's work. Practices such as taking time to appreciate nature, prayers or meditating every day
and mostly taking enough time to understand our emotions and
learning from past mistakes need dedication, time, perseverance

and patience. Yet, once you have mastered that art, you are unstoppable.

I know that courage comes in many forms. Once we start to open ourselves up, to reveal the part of ourselves that is soft and vulnerable, as well as strong, we find the courage to tell the truth and speak from the heart instead of the mind. We find the courage to have a voice – a voice that may have been lost through toxic people and environment, fear of outside judgement and lack of awareness. Through finding this courage, and stepping through fear, we become authentic to ourselves and to the outside world. We are no longer hiding in the shadows, locking up our true passionate selves.

For many women, both in my country, and elsewhere around the world, being authentic has been denied for so long by society. The power to speak from your heart openly and transparently is not something we are so good in doing and encouraging. We label those who are with being aggressive, overly open minded or different. We have a made-up catalogue of acceptable behaviours, phrases, actions and attitudes that we want all to conform with, especially women. Forgetting that women are the creators of life on this earth, and the real architects of society. But power comes from within. I have learned to listen to my intuition; I know my own truth and I am not afraid to speak it. It is only through awakening my curiosity that I can find that courage within myself.

I have learned to listen better to my rationale side. To better listen to what my heart, mind and body are telling me. I have learned to understand my limitations and use them to my advantage. I have learned when to let people in and when to say no. I have learned who to let go. I have learned what belongs to my world and what does not. From bad diets to bad relationships, addictions, habits, conversations and attachments that shut us off and mask who we truly are I have learned that it is okay to let go of these destructive forces that surround me. Instead, I have told myself that I deserve to surround myself with people who nourish me intellectually and spiritually and help me to grow.

Most of all, I have admitted that if fear can hold me back, it can surely transform me and free my soul. Once I recognised my life story had been ruled by fear for so long, I could begin to liberate myself from it.

I also made peace with the idea of perfectionism–that I am not perfect. No one is, and no one actually wants to be perfect, it is such a heavy burden to carry around.

Courage is not handed to us. Instead, it is a discovery process within while we peel the layers of our journey of life. It is the discovery of our purest and deepest layers within our hearts.

My nineteenth learning: Knowing who we are, actually living it, and proudly showing it to others are some of the most courageous acts we can experience. These are all forms of courage to celebrate.

Reflect and relate: Describe some forms of personal courage that you have experienced.

> Courage is not a special quality reserved for selective human beings. No person on earth was born a courageous person. It is developed through facing the things we fear.

_____

_____

_____

_____

_____

_____

_____

_____

_____

_____

Stepping Stone Twenty: Dancing with Fear Every Now and Then

"Life is found in the dance between your deepest desire and your greatest fear."

—Tony Robbins, Public Speaker, Life Coach and Philanthropist

Story twenty: Living fearlessly is not a life lived without fear at all. To live with fear is to be human. The anxieties we have about who we are, our place in society, our relationship with God, to mention a few, are all part of our very existence. But it is when we are trapped in fear that we lose who we are; we disappear as it engulfs us and freezes us. Instead, I found ways to dance with fear every now and then and move through it. I embraced it as a friend rather than resist it, and I found it turns into a good listener.

I spoke before about the fire-walk that I took part in during my training to become a life coach. That one single act encapsulated the fear that I had been living with for so long. Before I could place one step after the other I had to overcome so much including the life-changing burns I had experienced as a toddler. The act of walking across scalding hot coals in itself became a powerful symbol of my journey. I was moving through fear.

I have learned that fear was not going to paralyse me, like a sickness creeping through my body. Now, I wake up each morning thinking that whatever the world throws at me there is always a solution and a reason for it. I see fear now as a catalyst for growth rather than a reason to hold me back.

This does not mean that I want to live with fear day-in and day-out, even if it has become a good listener. Fear can erode a person. It can eat into their very organs. But healthy fear, the kind of fear we have when we are on the cusp of changing our lives, can propel us forward if only we learn how to channel that fear positively.

These challenges, or as I like to call them "eye-opening moments," still exist as part of living, but I have learned to deal with these differently. Instead of resisting, I embrace the fresh experience of solving the problem and the lessons that come with such experience.

The moment I experience fear in my gut, I step back and practice mindful breathing. With every breath my anxieties start to melt away. With this practice I am turning my focus inside rather than outside and giving myself those few minutes of quick grounding. Nature as well plays a vital role in my life to overcome my fears. Through taking time out to walk surrounded by nature, I feel connected again to life – a life bigger than me, and a life of God's making. While breathing my fears away I started noticing the power of acknowledgement. Acknowledging what you feel and the emotions you are having. I just notice them now, and let them wash over me rather than spending days, weeks, months or even years massively hiding those feelings or entertaining them. Now I thank them that they are here and let them go. I have learned to know that this moment right now is the most precious moment I have, and that this moment will also pass. It is up to me how and on what I want to spend it. I have learned that I am not made up of the thoughts that ebb and flow from moment to moment, day to day, month to month and year to year. I am not defined by them as far as I do not let them. Nor I am defined by other people's thoughts – the labels they have placed on me, the limitations of who they think I am or want me to be.

By facing my fears head-on rather denying their existence, and adopting beliefs that empower me and fuel my faith it became easier to do the dance with enjoyment instead of resistance.

My twentieth learning: We are gifted as human beings and as species by being resilient and adaptable by nature. We are not only shaped by things going well, but our lives are also shaped by the most difficult times. Each one of us has a part deep down that is strong and courageous. Call on that part and step up every time you are experiencing fear.

Reflect and relate: When fear hits you, what techniques do you use to calm your mind and soul?

> Dance through life. When you dance, your purpose is not to get to a certain place on the floor. It is to enjoy each step along the way – Dr. Wayne W. Dyer

---

3

LOVE – THE TRUTH

"A deep sense of love and belonging is an irreducible need of all people. We are biologically, cognitively, physically, and spiritually wired to love, to be loved, and to belong. When those needs are not met, we don't function as we were meant to. We break. We fall apart. We numb. We ache. We hurt others. We get sick."

—*Brene Brown, Researcher, Author and Storyteller*

Stepping Stone Twenty-One: A Lost *Fairy Tale*

> *"Let there be spaces in your togetherness, and let the winds of the heavens dance between you. Love one another but make not a bond of love: Let it rather be a moving sea between the shores of your souls. Fill each other's cup but drink not from one cup. Give one another of your bread but eat not from the same loaf. Sing and dance together and be joyous, but let each one of you be alone, Even as the strings of a lute are alone though they quiver with the same music. Give your hearts, but not into each other's keeping. For only the hand of Life can contain your hearts. And stand together, yet not too near together: For the pillars of the temple stand apart, And the oak tree and the cypress grow not in each other's shadow."*

—*Gibran Khalil Gibran, Poet, Writer and Artist*

Story twenty-one: The water was still dripping from the shower as I lay on the bathroom floor and I watched as each drop made its way down onto the slippery floor. My mind was as foggy as the steamy air but somehow I navigated through the pain, confusion and hurt of a lost fairy tale. As I lay there, the vision of me dancing my way to school, counting the jagged pavements while my ponytails swung from side to side, sprang to mind. I remembered what my mother told me every morning: "Rana, do not talk to strangers, they might harm you and you are still young. You would not be able to defend yourself." I would reply in disbelief: "But why would anyone want to hurt me?" Falling in love for me was, and still is, a state of being, so it was natural for me to fall in love and get married. With time, I started losing myself in pursuit of a false dream, a fairy tale. I have chosen marriage and vowed that only till death do us part. I started wondering about those vows. So many of us make them when we embark on a life of promise with a partner. But are we obliged to continue this sacred unity even when it loses its reason for being? Is death the only reason for us to part? What about adultery? Mental and physical abuse? Emotional blackmail? Married people might go through all these heartaches. What about shocking realities? What about mismatching values and visions? And what about the death of love, passion, compassion and tranquillity? Why are we tricked into believing that death comes only in a physical form?

We lose ourselves when we give too much for too long without nurturing the inner soul. That night, all I could focus on was the ugly orange pattern of the shower curtain. "How on earth did I choose such a colour?" I thought. I have never liked orange: it is one of those colours that has no identity, in my opinion. "You are not a yellow, nor a red," I thought. "You are a confused colour! Just like me." "Have an identity, orange! Stand up for yourself!" I was screaming inside. I was so angry at orange that I wanted to rip it from the rainbow chart. Suddenly, it occurred to me. I was not angry at orange, I was angry at myself, at the orange in me. When did I allow myself to lose my identity? When was being powerless become the new me? From that moment, it struck me that something had to change. I had to find the courage to bring my bold and bright red identity back and take control of my life. I let myself drift to sleep, and for the first time for so long, I slept with a smile and found a glimpse of light on the horizon and enough courage to wake up another day.

My twenty-first learning: Love with all your heart, but when that love does not serve you and there is no hope, choose a new direction. Do not let your life be a cycle of pain while you chase a lost fairy tale.

Reflect and relate: Have you ever lost your identity while in a relationship?

Some tips to avoid losing your identity in a relationship:

- Invest in yourself and your passions;
- Keep your friends close by;
- Stay connected with your family;
- Set your boundaries quickly.

_____

_____

_____

_____

_____

_____

_____

_____

Stepping Stone Twenty-Two: Self-Love: Where Is That?

"The surest way to lose your self-worth is by trying
to find it in the eyes of others."

—*Becca Lee, Writer*

Story twenty-two: I did not know what self-love was or how to find it before. Many people, especially women, spend their lives on a continuous circle of pleasing others. We as wives, mothers, daughters, and friends are told from an early age to put others first. Not understanding that taking care of ourselves first is the first step to understand self-love, or the lack of it. But self-love is confusing. If we nurture ourselves, are we being selfish? I was always so afraid of making sure I was okay. I worried about what people would think, or that they would criticise me. I was scared that my sons would not understand why I was not with them or that any potential partner would not love me for who I was. Saying "No" felt so counterintuitive to my whole being, as if my heart was being wrenched and twisted every time. Guilt consumed me. From an early age, we are seeking acceptance and love from the outside world. We want to make our parents proud, our teachers proud, our managers proud, our kids and our partners proud too. What an exhausting way of living! Forgetting that the first step to any great love story starts with self-love. I became exhausted by the constant treadmill of pleasing, pleasing and more pleasing, unable to press pause or even see what I was doing. Yet taking time off to nurture myself felt strange, indulgent even, perhaps even arrogant. If I loved myself so much then what if people sensed me as unreachable? It took me time to understand that self-respect and self-love are two sides of the same coin. The more you respect your time, your energy, your connection with God and your positive connection with the world around you, the more that bowl of self-love will be filled. Instead of a destructive circle, it becomes a virtuous one. Little by little, I started taking some time out for myself. Even if it was just half an hour every day to sit on the sofa and just be still, I learned to relax. I learned to let the day's stresses drain from me. I learned that it was okay to wind down and not be perfect or pretend to be all the time. That half an hour has extended to proper nurturing time for walking, reading, writing, reflection, meditation and so on. It is time for me to appreciate the small things in life and to feel gratitude for all things I have – my boys, my family, my health, my friends, the people I love and the beautiful world around me. Most of all, it is time for me to feel a closer connection and love with myself. Slowly I allowed myself to be nurtured with less guilt. "I drew on my bathroom mirror using my red lipstick: I love you," and kept it there for a while as my morning reminder to nourish myself more, and express love to myself first before others. With this, self-love was starting to become more familiar as the days passed by.

My twenty-second learning: You can spend all your life searching for self-love. You can reflect yourself in unfulfilled relationships, toxic friendships and environments that drain you and stop you from prospering on the false assumption that self-love resides there. Self-love begins and ends with you. Self-love is a daily practice.

Reflect and relate: What is self-love for you?

Five examples in practicing self-love:

- Buy yourself fresh flowers;
- Take time to rest and relax;
- Be patient with yourself;
- Celebrate your wins and stop the comparison;
- Learn to say "No."

_____

_____

_____

_____

_____

_____

_____

_____

_____

Stepping Stone Twenty-Three: To Give or Not to Give? That Was Always the Question

"I aspire to be a giver – a giver of love, a giver of good vibes and a giver of strength."

—*Anonymous*

Story twenty-three: I am like my mother. When I was younger I did not recognise it, but as I have grown older that fact has become clearer to me. My mother cares about everybody. She cares about people she does not even know. If I tell her now a friend is ill, she would ring me to ask if that friend is okay. She cannot sleep if she knows someone is in pain. Love is the very core of her being: it united us as a family, helped us, guided and nurtured us. This strategy worked for my mother well before my father was diagnosed with cancer; he had a heart attack when he was in his early forties. She nursed him, cared for him, loved him and he loved her for that. Their long marriage was successful, and she was heartbroken when my father finally passed away. I suppose I learned from her example, saw her life as a recipe for success and emulated her behaviour, regardless of whether people nurtured me back. As a passionate child, and now as an adult, I never held back about how I felt. I never held back from giving everything away all at once. I see it in my eldest son too. He has the same fire in his heart, the same burning love for people. It is his instinct to take care of people, just as it is his grandmother's and his mother's. But this desire can cause a dilemma. I have been constantly pulled between whether to give or not to give, or how much to give. I run into life giving away too much of myself, while others hold back. Every time I meet a new friend, lover or colleague, even a stranger I give away love, time and energy, never worrying about whether life is being drained from me. Over time, I have understood why I am like this. I give because this is who I am. I will always give because it is the right thing to do. It connects me with God and I know that what I receive from God fills me with more love and kindness that can spill out to others. But, when does giving actually drain your soul? When do you become stuck in a cycle of giving and not receiving? Does it mean you stay in relationships that are not working? Does it mean you let others walk all over you? This dilemma, this cycle, became an addiction. Just like sugar, junk food, sex or alcohol that people need as a way to run away from reality. So, I would fill myself up with pleasing people, then shut myself down when I was drained and under detox. When I had more energy I was again back to it and the cycle would continue. I went through times of mistrusting my own judgement about who I let into my life. I would tell myself maybe I am expecting too much from people around me, maybe I am forgetting that I am enough. Though I could not stay cold-hearted for long, when the detox ended, giving flowed from me like a river and I was back in the same place, stuck in the same cycle. Every time I gave too much and became hurt by it, I vowed again that I would not care about people. But this punished me more because this is against human nature. We as humans are givers by nature regardless of the walls we build around ourselves to protect us. Some people keep those walls up all their lives and keep playing the hide-and-seek game, while others choose to break free and fly away, freeing their natural being. I belong to this group. So, when my heart became a prisoner with my empath locked inside of me, desperate to break free, I had to find a way to channel this part of me in meaningful ways. Through a greater understanding of who I am and what my limits are, I have found ways to give that helped me evolve and grow rather than suffocated me. Through trial and error, I have been able to break free from the unhealthy chains of giving and pleasing people and started to nurture the giver in me in ways that are healthy for me and the people around me. I have buried the old pattern of unhealthy giving and have risen above that need: stronger, aligned and kinder in a most beautiful way with no attachments, expectations or excuses.

My twenty-third learning: Recognise when you are trapped by giving. Our greatness is not in what we have but in what we can give, yet when that is stopping us and holding us back from life, then it will be the right time to start seeking a changed behaviour.

Reflect and relate: Ask yourself: "How can I break out from my unhealthy giving patterns? How can I give without losing myself?"

Some healthy habits of giving:

- Spending quality time with others;
- Enrol yourself in a charity;
- Being emotionally available without losing yourself;
- Donate your books to others;
- Make someone laugh.

Stepping Stone Twenty-Four: Intimacy

> *"No relationship can truly grow if you go on holding back.*
> *If you remain clever and go on safeguarding and protecting*
> *yourself, only personalities meet, and the essential centres*
> *remain alone. Then only your mask is related, not you.*
> *Whenever such a thing happens, there are four persons in the*
> *relationship, not two. Two false persons go on meeting, and*
> *the two real persons remain worlds apart."*

> —*Osho, Leader and Mystic*

Story twenty-four: What is the ultimate expression of intimacy? How do we know when we have reached it? So many of us understand only the physical aspect to be the ultimate expression of true love, but there is so much more than this. Holding hands, kissing and making love are all part of intimacy, but real intimacy encompasses understanding who we are and being comfortable with ourselves. Only then we can bring intimacy into our relationships.

Others may think that intimacy is being with someone all of the time, clinging to them with our fingernails for every second we are in their company, as if tomorrow they will disappear and will be lost to us.

But I view intimacy as giving each other space and coming together for inspiring conversations. It is about looking at the stars together, walking on the beach, taking in the beauty of life with the one person who is special to you. Intimacy is about being still with each other and igniting each other's souls. It is about never being afraid of sharing ideas, opinions and mostly your emotions.

It is about enjoying the time, the moments rather than being competitive and desperate to win the argument with the other. This is the intimacy that you will not always see in fairy tales or films, but this is the very lifeblood of a relationship: this is its heartbeat, its pulse. When you know you can share anything with your partner, you can just be you: an embodiment of everything that you are or are not.

Because of my work, travels and the way my life has turned out to be so far, I am always on the move from one place to another. Hence not being physically present with my sons, my family and the people I love all the time, I have come to understand intimacy in different ways, and to find new ways of connecting. I have had to snatch moments of time and adapt to this new, strange yet fulfilling way of living. I have had to share some precious moments over a laptop screen, or through video calls, or by a text, never touching, hugging or feeling a person physically to realise that connection. This is something the world has faced during the COVID-19 pandemic. Finding new ways to connect, sharing our love, kindness and empathy has never been tested before as in these times. Opening our hearts and souls to new forms of intimacy can be frightening at certain points, but what matters is how you make people feel, and there are millions of ways to make them feel loved, mattered and appreciated.

To experience all of that, I have had to strip back the version of myself that I presented to the world. I have had to show my vulnerability, show that I cry, that I do feel and that I am not strong all the time. I have had to accept that these are all part of me, parts that have been trodden down or that I have suppressed as I lost more of myself. Furthermore, I realised that intimacy is about seeing my bad side as well as my good, not just the part that suits at any given moment. I have learned to love them unconditionally, and while I am doing that, I am trusting that someone will reciprocate that unconditional self-love I have for all my parts and will vibrate at the same level with me. Intimacy can then become the complete acceptance of someone's own feelings.

But intimacy is a walk, not a race. We cannot hope to find intimacy straight away; rather it is a process of trust-building, souls finding and passion igniting. It is about finding the courage to tell someone who you are, what you want from life, what your hopes and dreams are. It is about fearlessly opening your heart to love, but knowing that if that love hurts you, you have the power to express your feelings still and cherish them because they are a part of you. It is about knowing that you do not have to present a false version of yourself. And, it is about knowing that you have the power to leave. I realised that you can tell many people in your life that you love them. Nevertheless, the most important words that you can say or hear from someone is not "I love you" but "I can be myself around you." That is intimacy for me. Intimacy can be so grand, pure and fulfilling when it is the connection of the souls: it is the alchemy of all relationships.

My twenty-fourth learning: It is only when you bring your authentic self to a relationship that true intimacy happens. Intimacy is being with someone with whom you can be yourself fully and who ignites your soul by just being themselves.

Reflect and relate: Here is your safe space to ask yourself what kind of intimacy you want in your life, and dig deep to find the answers.

> There are four types of intimacy:
>
> • Emotional, mental, spiritual and physical. Each one has different ways of expression.

_____

_____

_____

_____

_____

_____

_____

_____

_____

Stepping Stone Twenty-Five: Protect My Boundaries, but How?

"Daring to set boundaries is about having the courage to love ourselves even when we risk disappointing others."

—*Brené Brown, Researcher and Author*

Story twenty-five: I had found boundaries difficult: setting them, understanding them and protecting them. Shutting myself off to someone, or telling them I cannot give them the love and the support they need, or just not being there for them because I was incapable of doing so had caused me deep pain. This had happened in relationships, friendships and even with family. It was difficult through the early steps of my journey in life to fully comprehend that I am a separate being from those people around me. I could not simply immerse myself in their own needs and neglect mine. Because of this, I had, even unconsciously, allowed people to walk over my boundaries, at times to the point where I lost all sense of what they were.

I also never really took the time to understand what my boundaries were. I did not know where to start, or maybe I was at times too complacent to start the search. In the chaos of life, the storm of heartbreak and loss, I did not tune into my feelings. I did not connect with my inner soul. I did not name proudly and loudly my limits or boundaries. Instead, I moulded into other peoples' characters rather than asking: Who am I? What do I really want? What am I prepared to give? What is right for me? What do I want to share?

Losing all sense of my boundaries seemed unfamiliar to me, yet at times I fully lost it. Was it guilt that consumed me as an adult? Or, confusion between kindness and my right to say no that led me to be available all the time to everyone and anyone to share a piece of my mind, heart and soul, until each cell of me begged me to stop and set my boundaries, my limits and my rules.

Armed with my new antenna, I started walking through life alert, not dulled by everything that was going on around me. I saw the danger signs, like an animal in the wild vigilant to a predator: those people happy to take from me but unwilling to give. And when I began to see these markers of potential abuse, neglect or unsupportive relationships, I suddenly found my voice, a voice that had been silent for so long, that could not speak the words of love, only of fear. Suddenly, I became my authentic self simply by setting my own boundaries and living by them daily.

I could not put a fence up around my heart – a barrier to love. I never wanted to. Instead, I have learned to navigate a path. I have learned to set a balance and have direct answers. I have learned how to say, "No, I do not want to go out," or "I do not want to do this," or "I am too tired to address this now." I have learned to say "no" without explanation. I have learned that "no" by itself is a complete sentence. I started to give off my time in a way that was right for me. I wrote down my non-negotiable boundaries, the things I would not be able to tolerate, that would interrupt my spiritual connection to God or would harm others. Then, I listed those scenarios I could be more flexible with, alongside those I was happy to indulge more in. Knowing your boundaries is part of knowing yourself and revealing your authentic self to the world. I define an authentic person as being a powerful force. They listen to their intuition; they know their truth and are not afraid to speak it. They create a life and live within the rules they created for themselves and not by the book. They are curious and question everything, and they recognise what belongs in their world and what does not. They are not afraid to say no and know exactly when to say yes, and they are not afraid to let go. They are passionate about what they believe in and fight for.

I discovered that setting my own boundaries makes me real and even more approachable.

My twenty-fifth learning: We all have a set of rules that identify us. With this insight, we would know what our boundaries are and know when they are being stepped on. If those boundaries are crossed, find the courage to speak up and learn how to protect them.

Reflect and relate: When will you awaken your authentic self, give that person air to breathe and room to grow? When is it the right time to set your own boundaries?

Tips: You are entitled to your own thoughts and opinions

You are entitled to your own feelings to a given situation.
You are entitled to your own space, however wide that may look to others;
You are entitled to your own spiritual beliefs.

_____

_____

_____

_____

_____

_____

_____

_____

Stepping Stone Twenty-Six: The Different Sides of Me

*"My mission in life is not merely to survive, but to thrive;
and to do so with some passion, some compassion, some
humour, and some style."*

—*Maya Angelou, Poet, Singer, Memoirist and Civil Rights
Activist*

Story twenty-six: I could not figure out the different sides of me at once, although the toughness and softness were both present at younger age. All these different aspects of my personality were waiting to be expressed, yet I could not give them all avenues for expression.

It is funny that as a little girl I had dreamt of being an actress. I dressed up and played out my dream to be on stage, not really knowing that I was experimenting with all the different parts of my character. Every person has such different versions of characters in them, yet so many of us have not yet discovered them or befriended them.

Over the past few years, I have learned that I can be a mass of contradictions. I can be serious and studious, but playful. I can be romantic, passionate yet funny and quirky. I can be a lady boss and compassionate at the same time, spiritual but adventurous, and my role in my journey of life is to embrace all these characters, and nurture each one of them separately or collectively.

Perhaps it is because my zodiac sign is Virgo that I have such contradictory sides. Being an earth sign, we are reliable, practical and solid – the backbone of the zodiac. We are blessed with intelligence but cursed with self-criticism and judgement. We can turn the laser beam of perceptiveness on others and the world around us, but we mostly direct it at ourselves. My savage inner judge knows no bounds. At times I can soar to the heights of achievements and fulfilment, while that the side of self-criticism wants to crawl back in to ruin the moment. Now, I stop it from holding me back.

But how many of us actually sit with ourselves and see all of our different sides? How many of us want to know more about ourselves? We are so consumed of wanting to know the outside world that we tend to forget to look inside and not just to look, but to look with an understanding eye and an accepting heart. Often we are too scared to see, scared to express who we are for fear of unpleasant discoveries. But knowing ourselves is a revolving process as any discovery. As I write this book, the world is gripped by a pandemic. Anxiety and panic permeate every part of society and every country. I myself had to be isolated and confined alone. As the hours ticked by in my hotel room, I thought, "What if I died now and no one knew who I was? What if I died and people never knew the kindness in my heart? The funny side in me? Or the loving and passionate human being? What if I am not able to show the real me ever again?"

When you know all your different sides you realise you are part of God's wonderful creation, and you have some aspects in your character that resembles others. You start to embrace love and nurture every aspect.

My twenty-sixth learning: Spend some time every day on getting to know yourself. It is acceptable to have different contradicting sides of your character. They make the real you, and that real in you is unique.

Reflect and relate: Dedicate half an hour every day to discover parts of you that are hidden, whether accepting a new challenge, discovering a new hobby or just being still and listening to yourself.

> Different people we meet in our lives bring out different sides of us.

_____

_____

_____

_____

_____

_____

_____

_____

_____

_____

Stepping Stone Twenty Seven: What Is Love?

*"A life without love is of no account. Don't ask yourself what
kind of love you should seek, spiritual or material, divine or
mundane, Eastern or Western. Divisions only lead to more
divisions. Love has no labels, no definitions. It is what it is,
pure and simple. Love is the water of life. And a lover is a soul
of fire! The universe turns differently when fire loves water."*

—*Shams Al-Tabrizi, Sufi and Mystic*

Story twenty-seven: I have always been a lover, and I have been
always fascinated by what love is. I fell in love with God, a partner
and my family, and I can fall head over heels, day after day, with
a new passion or an exciting idea. I fall in love with nature and
with all God's creatures. Mainly I rise with love, the love for other
people's souls.

I am only the best version of myself when I am in love with everything and anything unconditionally. When I am in love, I am in
love with all. True love for me is love without expectations. Love
is inclusive. Love does not differentiate. Love unites. We own love:
it is our natural rightful emotion as human beings. Love and life
move in tandem together. Love and only love can guide us home
to where we actually belong and to what we truly are.

But at certain points in my life I could not love one or more of these
things fully and completely. And, just like me before, so many of
us want to give up on love. We become hurt and crawl into a deep
hole where we put up our defences, shield ourselves from the pain
of the world and let nothing into our hearts.

At the time when I was questioning everything, I could not see that love was all around me. I could not wake up every day feeling joy at the world. The more I opened myself up to life, the more love flooded in, as if I had opened a window to my soul and let the sunbeams dance inside of me. Love moves within my veins as oxygen does by adding more life to life itself.

We sometimes have a limited view of love. We box into the narrow confines of marriage and a partnership. There are so many more forms of love, the love of family, friends, humanity and more. Motherhood is as well one of the purest forms of love; the love I have for my sons is a love like no other. It soars and swoops like a bird in flight. Whenever I see them and talk to them, open my arms to them and hug them my heart leaps.

When I walk in the afternoon and see the blossom appearing on the trees and the heart shapes in the clouds, I know that love is everywhere. Love is hope, connection, acceptance of ourselves and other people.

Even if love is not tangible at times we should never give up on love. We owe it to ourselves to work towards fostering openness in our hearts. This energy will glow from you and this love will create more love. Love is magnetic. It pulls in positivity from all around. If we first focus our energy on making ourselves happy and if we can fill our hearts with the emotions of love, then we can love others equally, passionately and wholly and attract all forms of love into our own beings.

Math did not ignite my interest much in high school. But recently when I was contemplating the formula of life, one observation that kept me curious was that the more I add fear to the equation of life, the more its equation gets whacked and out of balance. The least I get out of life. So I tried and tested until I observed a pattern with satisfactory results by adding more love. With that formula, life itself started showing me more lives to the original equation to discover, more components to add and interestingly new codes to test and play with exquisitely. When there is more love inside, there will be less fear.

My twenty-seventh learning: Love is the force of life. It motivates us if we open our hearts to love. Then love becomes our natural state.

Reflect and relate: If you want to describe what is love for you, what would you say?

My love poem to You:

"My heart beats to the rhythm of love.
I didn't fall in love with you.
I flied higher loving you.
My wings are wide open, choosing to take every step along
    the way.
I do believe in fate and destiny, but I also believe that some
    connections defy common sense, reasoning or gravity.
Our heartbeats rhyme in synchronisation
Knowing deep inside that this love story is the ultimate
    realisation."

_____

_____

_____

_____

_____

_____

Stepping Stone Twenty-Eight: The Magic Pill for Successful Relationships

> *"The greatest gift you can give any partner-past, present or future is to be so connected with who you truly are that they are irrelevant to your connection. And when they are irrelevant to your connection, then you are going to have a really good time together."*

> —*Abraham Hicks, Speaker and Author*

Story twenty-eight: I used to believe that my prince would come, bend on one knee and ask me to marry him. We would have children, a beautiful house and we would live happily ever after. I thought that someone else, a man, would complete me. He would gather up all my pieces and make me whole, or more complete.

If I think about this now, it is a crazy notion. No one can make another person whole, and through my previous marriage I came to realise that. What a responsibility to place on another person. What a path of unfulfilled happiness we are storing up for ourselves. Only we can look inside our souls and nurture our pieces, even the broken ones. Only we can understand our past fully and can view ourselves with compassion and wholeness. Only we can propel ourselves forward and fulfil our hopes and dreams. Only we can learn to live with fear and use it as a catalyst for growth, by using it to our best advantage and by making life work for us. The other person is not here to complete me, or you; they are here to complement us and there is a huge difference between both. After a relationship goes wrong, many of us shy away from meeting someone new. Instead, we lick our wounds, unsure of whether we can trust and be trusted to venture out into the world again to meet our heavenly match. But it should never put us off. I believe that people do find their soulmates, twin flames, our heavenly match, however you want to call them – our match is always out there somewhere. When our souls are complete, we meet as equals as we meet our partner with a complete self, and we are now ready to add meaning to our lives, and it is not for that relationship to be our only life. The secret is to have compassion and understanding for our separate journeys and nourish both equally. Our destination may be the same, but all of us will have taken a separate path individually. Our parents, siblings and even children are on their own path too. All we can do is assist a person on their journey, and instil in them the values of love and kindness.

It is the same with a partner. Removing the burden of responsibility means setting out clearly the expectations of the relationship. It is about communicating each other's needs and taking responsibility for our own emotional happiness. When I got divorced, I knew that repairing myself was a priority, that if I jumped into another relationship broken and incomplete, then my path would continue on the same circle, meeting at where it started – a point of destruction.

A solid relationship is about two whole people coming together because they love each other's company. It is about nurturing each other's talents, using love to free us to discover our true purpose in life. It is not about suffocating each other with love or needs. It is about bringing out the best in each other without expecting the other to add to our happiness. Rather, it is about discovering ourselves together through their eyes. It is about understanding all the parts of ourselves and bringing our wholehearted loving into a union.

My twenty-eighth learning: Unless you are a whole and complete person yourself, you will always attract a partner who is the reflection of that: not whole or complete. Dependency in this scenario is a recipe for disaster. The best relationships are those when neither is accountable for the happiness of the other, yet both are doing everything they can to add light, happiness and love to their lives together.

Reflect and relate: What is your recipe for a successful relationship?

Companionship
Communication
Support

Stepping Stone Twenty-Nine: Self-Love: I found YOU

> *"As I began to love myself I found that anguish and emotional suffering are only warning signs that I was living against my own truth. Today, I know, this is 'authenticity.' We no longer need to fear arguments, confrontations or any kind of problems with ourselves or others. Even stars collide, and out of their crashing new worlds are born. Today I know 'that is life.'"*

> *– Charlie Chaplin, Performer*

I used to think that self-love was the pursuit of external things. If only I had money, the best clothes, professional success and the best body, then I would find acceptance and admiration from others and transmit that into self-love. But as I began on the journey of loving myself, I came to understand that all these material things and aesthetics I was having were not the way to nurture my soul, nor were they anything close enough to let me discover the true meaning of self-love.

I used to think that self-love is the same as self-affection. Yes, I used to like myself and be fond of the things I do, the way I dress up, the places I go to and the people I interact with. I was fond of the best moments of my life. But was that self-love? What about my struggles, thoughts that keep me up all night, that burn scar on my chest, the grey hair that sometimes creeps every four weeks to remind me of my experiences in life? What about the mistakes I have made, the scars of the heart and those fearful moments that show up every time I am about to make a life-changing decision? Do I love all these as well as part of me, part of my version of self-love? The answer now is positively different. There were times when I could never have sat comfortably with myself, but this has changed. Life has forced me in different occasions to be with my only companion: my true self. Recently I realised how far I have come. While the world rages around me, I have been on my spiritual guidance and journey with God and feeling the love all inside of me, around me and through me. It is as if my reborn self is radiating out love from within to the world. Most of all those solitude times gave me the time to reflect on how much I have changed. I stopped looking around at lives that I perceived as better than mine – peering in at the window of others, longing that I should also live the perfect dream. I stopped trawling the internet, taking in snapshots of other people's happiness as if this was the truth. Instead I looked in and around me. What do I have? What could I appreciate more now? How could I grow better, humbler and truthful? I began to realise that without nurturing and connecting with my heart, my mind could travel to dark places. As I connected it to my heart, my mind became a valuable ally. I became wiser each and every day, and with that self-love ascended as a complete stand-alone component of my own happiness and fulfilment. I learned how to respect myself and others. I started to take care of what I eat, drink and expose myself to, to channel my self-love wisely. I began to protect my time. I kept working hard, succeeding and enjoying my career, but I did not do that to please or fulfil anyone's needs but myself. I decided not to use work as an escape, but rather part of my life combined with healthy moments of solitude and reflection. I also distanced myself from people in my life who drew energy from me and left me exhausted and drained in their company. I worked at being less competitive with others, or always trying to be right. Through this, I found a newfound modesty and realised that trying to be right drained my energy rather than boosting it. So I quit that pursuit, and, I concentrated on myself rather than trying to change others. I understood how unrealistic it is to force my desires on another person, especially if I know the time is not right and the person is not ready for it. Self-love allowed me to understand that it is safe for my heart to choose, and that I have the courage to love myself fully including my inner hidden pieces. It allowed me to feel the fullness of love, peace and pure joy inside of me and not feeling guilty if I am experiencing moments of full joy. It affirmed for me the fact that love radiates from me, around me and everywhere I go, and I would only encounter people and situations and go to places that have the same high vibrational energy of love. Self-love allowed me to understand fully now that love is my existing being and that my heart is such a beautiful organ.

My twenty-ninth learning: Self-love is the beginning and ending of all forms of love we encounter in our lives. It is the only path that leads us to redemption.

Relate and reflect: Did you love yourself today? And every day?

> "Be your best friend, your gym partner. Be your coffee bestie, and your partner in crime. Be everything for yourself rather than relying on others to be that for you." Those are some of my self-love conversations.

_____

_____

_____

_____

_____

_____

_____

_____

_____

_____

_____

Stepping Stone Thirty: The Bigger Picture

"As long as your curiosity is greater than your fear,
you will move forward!"

—*Mehmet Murat Ildan, Playwright, Novelist and Thinker*

Story thirty: Love is not what I expected it to be. We are told of God's love and the love between souls on earth, but until I began on my spiritual journey I did not understand the true power of love for God and how the connection with Him has given me the courage to change my own life and the strength to love and inspire others. At a time when the majority of the world's population is in lockdown, when we are unable to see our families, friends and loved ones, when we are confined to the four walls of hotel rooms and homes; when our loved ones are dying and we cannot even say our goodbyes, we need God's love more than ever. We understand now how each one's love and kindness can be part of the bigger picture of the universe's love. Times of tragedy unleash anguish like no other on the human heart. We inhale fear as if it were our last breath. We are suffocated with torment and suffering. But when we come through the darkness we realise love is everywhere and it is collective. It is in all the places we would least expect to find, if only we had looked for it.

My journey to explore love began with the lost fairy tale. Without a partner, I thought I could not survive. I had repeated my vows – till death do us part – in the eyes of God and I held on to that dream of love even when my heart was breaking and every day became a lie. I was lying to myself that unhappiness was what I had signed up for and I was lying to the people around me. I did not want to admit that love at one point had left me broken.

The hard decision to leave and file for divorce was one of the most painful and difficult decisions I have made in my life. No one wants to be seen as a failure, no one wants to break a family even for the benefit of our children, no one wants to feel abandoned and no one wants to navigate life alone with no companionship. It took every cell in me to be filled with courage to do that. But in so many ways it made me who I am now, and I am grateful for all of it. It allowed my wings to open and my soul to fly. It taught me never to settle. Slowly, and with new circumstances to navigate, I could let love back into my heart. But I did not find love always in the arms of another; I have found it immensely in the conversations I have with my sons, with my friends, my colleagues, with other human beings all around by looking outwards to the world, the love for our pets, nature and the life that God created for us. I found that I could give to people love, compassion, understanding and that my kindness could shine through, yet I could still be me without compromising, and I could still lead with love.

Our world will blossom when we choose love over fear. Daily peace and endless abundance come from choosing love and oneness, and forgiving everyone and everything. Once we free ourselves from our egos – as they judge, separate and cling helplessly on to harm – we experience the purest version of love: our existing natural force.

My thirtieth learning: Be amazed by the world around you, and when you allow yourself to see the world from a different angle, you start to see the bigger picture. We are not confined by our own tiny worlds. We are part of a larger creation. We all have our paths to walk along and our destinations to reach. Be compassionate with yourself and others as they make their way through life. Lead with love.

Reflect and relate: How do you usually express your love to others? Is there any different practice or way that you want to add or experience?

> I once asked a bird, "How is it that you fly in this gravity of darkness?" She responded, "LOVE LIFTS ME." – Hafiz

_____

_____

_____

_____

_____

_____

_____

_____

_____

_____

_____

4

LIGHT – THE WAY FORWARD

"If Light is in Your Heart, You Will Find Your Way Home."

—Rumi, Poet, Faqih, Islamic Scholar and Sufi Mystic

Stepping Stone Thirty-One: The Curious Little Girl in Me

"And those were seen dancing were thought to be insane by those who could not hear the music."

—*Nietzsche, Philosopher*

Story thirty-one: As soon as I understood how I could change, the rays of light started flooding back to my soul and into my life. I began to see life differently. I understood that the secret for healing was about removing the blockage in my mind – that blockage was fear. I did not live without fear; I learned how to overcome it and speak my truth. I had put on my helmet of perseverance and never stopped giving up on life. In turn, I became a more compassionate person: compassionate with myself, but with others too. Examining your past and forgiving yourself is such a powerful process. Every day, I approach the world with a different mindset – not one of judgement and hostility, but one of love, compassion and forgiveness. It is the same love and compassion and forgiveness I had shown as a child. Children have an amazing ability to bounce back when life weighs them down. As adults we can easily forget how to be adaptable to changing circumstances. Instead of using our agility as humans to find a new path, we resist, clinging on to old habits and toxic relationships as if our life depends on them. Yet children move on, adopt, become curious and they see the world through fresh eyes each time. From the moment I let the light back into my life, that little girl burst out of me once again. When I finished my life coaching course I started seeing the world in rainbow colours. It was my first step for me to see the other side of the coin and opened me to new dimensions I have not experienced before. The world becomes so vibrant around me and dancing with energy. I, too, was dancing inside. Even when challenges arose, I approached them differently. The little girl in me granted me calmness and focus. Through it all, I was so grateful to be alive. That is a blessing that so many people underestimate and one that I did, too. Having the chance to witness the beauty of another day is something that I cannot be more thankful for. As we get older and more fearful, we cling on to routine, too. These are the things we return to every day, even if they do not serve us well. When light flooded in I let go of humdrum routine. I saw the world as I saw myself: as a place to explore. I saw it through creative eyes. How could I nurture all the good and positive things inside of me? Must I continue on a path of marriage, work, children, outings and the same rhythm or routine that so many of us do? As I let go of some of the traditional structures in life that were not suitable for me, and started building my own brick after another, I become more fulfilled. And I started building a life inside my head that reminded me so much of the imaginary world I used to live in.

Whatever their surroundings, kids draw on energy around them. They drink in vitality and it spills out into the world. I started having ideas again like kids, being creative about how I approached life. If fear shook my foundation, which is a natural part of living, I faced it head-on, and I kept asking myself: "What would Rana, the little girl, do now? How does she feel? And who does she really want to be now?"

Soon, this positivity seeped into my daily life. Instead of seeing problems as what they are, I started seeing them as opportunities for me to learn something about me and about life itself. Each day was a blessing to be experienced. In turn, I took on more responsibilities and engaged in more activities that brought to my soul life. The small things in life became more manageable and enjoyable too. Believe it or not, it is those small things that can eat away the goodness in our hearts. Being stuck in a traffic jam or in a queue for our morning coffee or being late to that important meeting. Now, instead of experiencing those moments negatively, I enjoy the moment, flowing with it and through it. I notice the clouds as I wait; I notice the smile on the face of the beautiful lady making my coffee; I say hello to strangers. I notice other commuters on the way home. My steps resemble those of a vibrant dance. I have become open to the world around me just like I was as a happy, expressive and explorer child.

My thirty-first learning: The first step of awakening is to tap into your childlike self. True enlightenment is to forgive yourself and to live life through the eyes of a child.

Reflect and relate: What aspects of your childhood did you like the most? Can you bring some of them back into your current life?

> Our wild and child sides go hand in hand. Give room for both to be explored.

_____

_____

_____

_____

_____

_____

_____

_____

_____

_____

Stepping Stone Thirty-Two: On the Path to Enlightenment

"If God brings you to it, HE will bring you through it."

—Unknown

Story thirty-two: We can all talk the talk, but how do we make sure we walk it? On the path to enlightenment, I knew it was not enough to talk about being the best version of myself; I had to live and breathe it every day. It was not enough to read the Quran or pray; I needed to understand the meaning behind that. I needed to know why I was praying. My journey was towards having complete trust in God and His plan for me. Now I understood that every problem in life was part of His plan, that I am part of a wider universe than just my tiny world. I opened my soul and my heart to God and appreciated the beautiful part of questioning. My life started over again when gratitude filled my heart. I trusted that while there may be no answers, doors open to us as we navigate all of life's problems. It is in our power to steer a way through towards a better way of being. Then, I started connecting all the dots. I looked at all the heartbreaks that had happened to me. I looked at the universe around me and the part I wanted to play in it. I saw that through connection, I could be happy and serve others. Whatever happened, it was this connection that kept me focused on this path. Now, my daily routine includes sending two thankful prayers, one in the morning for giving me the chance to live another day, and the second one at night for guiding me through the day and giving me the chance to experiment and just be here. What I did not know when I started this book is that I would undergo another big test in my life. As I mentioned earlier, being quarantined as a result of the pandemic has become a symbol of how far I have come on my path to enlightenment. Could I turn this time of crisis and stress into a time of blessing and more enlightenment? Instead of shutting down my heart with fear, could I open up even more? Stuck in my hotel room, it was as if everything I had been thinking about and practicing came together. It was as if the years leading up to this moment were a rehearsal for life's great play. Now it was showtime. Had God been preparing me for this moment? How would I react? Would I let fear consume me? Or did the lessons actually register this time? Although there were times when staring at four bare walls was unbearable, alongside not being able to have long walks in the day as I always do, I took pleasure in small moments. From my balcony I could enjoy the azure blue of the waves, watch the trees swaying in the breeze and watch the sunrise and set, bathing the horizon in a golden hue. Was it fate that my room faced a beautiful sea? Was it planned that I could be mesmerised by the clouds and their shapes and the messages they were sending me again even while I am in confinement? I could not leave my room, but I sought to raise the spirit of others, whom I talked to while sitting in my balcony. I saw the beauty in what we were experiencing together. My morning meditation after my prayers took on a greater signifi- cance, another level too. I accepted that I was powerless to change what was happening. Instead of consuming myself with resistance and fear, it made me more humble, faithful, acceptable and flex- ible to my surroundings. I was more aware of my learnings and the test I have been blissfully part of. The experience by itself gave me unexpected peace in the mid of unprecedented chaos.

My thirty-second learning: We are all born to look towards light and hope. This gift is always in us and around us. Once you start towards the path of light you will turn every crisis into a blessing.

Reflect and relate: Where do you find hope in difficult times?

A glimpse into my soul:

I am light
I am peace
I am truth
I am healing
I am wonder
I am in constant metamorphosis
I am hope
I am love
I am infinite
I am nature

Stepping Stone Thirty-Three: Passion, Passion and More Passion

"The saddest people I've ever met in life are the ones who don't care deeply about anything at all. Passion and satisfaction go hand in hand, and without them, any happiness is only temporary, because there's nothing to make it last."

—*Nicholas Sparks, Novelist and Screenwriter*

Story thirty-three: Live with passion: it is the message that I have on a ring on my finger that I wear all the time. I brought it from the course I completed with life coach Tony Robbins, and it is there every day to remind me to live out my hopes and dreams and immerse myself in the moment. It is part of being the real me – my authentic self. It is who I am. Passion for me is the key driver for success: it supersedes skills and talents, as those can be taught, but you cannot teach someone to be passionate about an idea, goal or a purpose. You cannot teach someone to be passionate about life itself. You cannot teach someone to be enthusiastic, excited, proud, happy and love what they do. But you can advise them to be with themselves more. You can help them to connect with who they are, and give them the key to that door. It is then up to them to pursue life how they want with passion, or not. I see passion as the Emoji of the smiling face with two heart-shaped eyes. This is how your face looks like every morning when you wake up to pursue something you are excited about: that dream, vision, goal, idea or a purpose. Passion is that rare fire in your soul that makes you alive, and living with passion is a way of living that applies to everything and anything.

Nowadays, I do not hide my passion because hiding it would be such a destructive and selfish act for me and the people around me. Although, before I used to care so much whether what I am passionate about would be acceptable to others, the current trend, the norm or meet certain expectations. Today, I wear my passion with pride. So what if what interests me in life is different from those of my friends? What if I am passionate about many different things at the same time? What if I have my own formula of living passionately? With time, I have learned to talk about them, to express my thoughts about the things that keep me in wonderment regardless of what people think. By doing this, I have found that it is not me who has found passion; instead it has found me. I talked before about finding pleasure in everyday things and how, since basking in rays of light, my perspective changed. I even wake up with love and energy, ready for what the day will bring. In this mindset, positivity sticks to me like a magnet. People around me see that I am comfortable with who I am, and living my passions makes them comfortable too. People feel comfortable, even if they hide it, around others who are true to themselves because they know they do not have to play the game of pretending or faking. I have never wanted to change people; as mentioned before it is not my responsibility or yours to change anyone. It is our responsibility though to live up to our values and what we believe in. That by itself inspires others. I have been inspired by so many people in my life, and still I am, every single day. Every person you meet can add to your experience positively or negatively depending on what you want to absorb. Living fully is about putting everything into living life. I do not believe in half measures or half efforts. For me this is not about making money, having fame, material things or achieving status. It is about the feeling of fulfilment I have inside – that feeling of comfort and pleasure that comes from giving my all and knowing

I have done my part, and that I have the best intentions in life. I know maybe it is not easy to comprehend how someone could be passionate and excited about life when it is hard and we are faced by calamity all around. I understand that, but I understand as well that it is a choice we make. I know I sometimes make my colleagues laugh and wonder when they ask me: "What drugs are you on today that make you excited, Rana?" or "What are you so excited about every morning?" It can be hard sometimes to explain that I am high on life itself and the only drug I am on is the Drug of Life. The best part of living life with passion is that it always pays off. What you put in, you get back. It means that whatever happens, you have not compromised yourself. I know I have not been a cold, dull person, cowed by the judgements of what is normal, trending or easy to do. I have not settled. I have found a way to live my best life. And, most of all, I am enjoying living this life. I am thriving, not just surviving.

My thirty-third learning: Being passionate means you are fully immersed in any experience. It becomes not about the end result, but the process of that experience that gives you joy and satisfaction and teaches you lessons along the way.

Reflect and relate: Find something that you care deeply about and nurture that idea.

Five keys to living a passionate life:

- Be honest with yourself;
- Find your passion;
- Learn to deal with resistance;
- Enjoy what you are doing;
- Find the interaction between what you love to do, what you are good at and what people are willing to pay for.

Stepping Stone Thirty-Four: Authentic Me – Can I Dare?

"To be nobody-but-yourself – in a world which is doing its best, night and day, to make you everybody else means to fight the hardest battle which any human being can fight; and never stop fighting."

—*E. E. Cummings, Poet and Author*

Story thirty-four: "I have to be a true voice for myself." I kept repeating this day in day out. For many years, I had not wanted people to see the real me, afraid that these vulnerabilities would be used against me. I was not perfect too. I was beautifully flawed just like everybody else, only now I am not afraid to admit it. Looking back, I admit, I had acted rashly sometimes without taking care of myself and nurturing my inner soul. I was not kind enough. But admitting this and forgiving myself for these moments have empowered me.

I have always been faced with two options in life: to be how others want me to be, or be myself. I feel as if the universe keeps pushing me towards choosing myself every single time. Until I really got it one day that being myself is the most courageous act I can do. Choosing myself was my reflection of choosing life itself. Whereas before it was so important for me to be liked, now I only want to be liked by people who understand all of me – the good and the bad. Being on the merry-go-round of trying to be someone I am not and being the person society wants me to be is exhausting. Pursuing an ideal of perfection is exhausting too. Yet so many people do this, whether it is the perfect house, job, relationship or body. We are all guilty of wanting to attain things that do not fulfil us, purely to fit with that glittery show we enrolled in. Instead, authenticity has given me peace of mind. I know that I do not want to hide behind a false version of myself, like an actress on a stage. I want to play the starring role in my life, understanding all the parts where I have succeeded and the parts that need improvement. I see myself as a constantly evolving universe, my own planet that can adapt and change as the sun rises and sets within the larger solar system.

By seeing myself as a work in progress, I can reach out to others and help them along their journey to authenticity. I can guide people to understand that they are also perfect in their imperfections. We all have fears and aspirations; we are all connected regardless of whatever stage or age we are in life. It is in finding this connection with God and with each other that will help us wind the thread of life back to who we are in our hearts.

My thirty-fourth learning: You will be surprised at how showing the real you and being authentic is inspiring to others. So many of us are afraid of showing our true selves to the world, but once we find our true voice it can liberate us and others on the way.

Reflect and relate: How do you define an authentic person?

> Courage is to follow what is authentic within you.

_____

_____

_____

_____

_____

_____

_____

_____

_____

_____

_____

_____

Stepping Stone Thirty-Five: More Life

"My purpose in life is to make one person happier a day."

—Rana Abu Samaha, Human Being

Story thirty-five: My purpose in life is to make one person happier a day. It is part of the reason I decided to learn more about coaching, our minds and energy. Over the past few years, I have been fascinated at how we create versions of ourselves in our minds that do not match up to the reality. When we do not achieve the ideal of who we think we should be, we punish ourselves.

I started the movement of More Life by Rana – coaching and serving through inspirational app and quotes couple of years ago. Every day, I realised that we can serve and help others in different ways, that even at my corporate day-to-day work, I can still fulfil my purpose by being there for people, listening, connecting, collaborating and engaging fully with others and by serving other human beings. As long as I know what my purpose is, the universe keeps directing me towards fulfilling it. My eyes have started opening to new possibilities and new ways of living. I remember a time when I wanted to talk and see my own point of view only. I walked around surrounded by only my own thoughts. I was blinkered to the outside world and to the wisdom that shone all around me. I was blind to the path He was leading me on. As my curiosity awakened once more, and I became humble, I started listening to others. I wanted to know what gems of wisdom they could bring to my world and to this universe. How could they guide me, and contribute to my life, and how could I do the same to them? By reengaging with my passions, I found my purpose. I am a natural empath, someone who wants to help others to be their best selves. This time, I approached this with the wisdom I had gathered through my life's experiences. Instead of being drained by kindness, I was mindful to understand my own boundaries. Having a purpose and also a sense of control over my own emotions and thoughts made me feel more balanced. It is as if everything that was out-of-kilter in my life slowly found an equilibrium.

Exploring my interests such as becoming a life coach, reading more, learning about energy, spiritual connection, nature, the universe, striking up conversations with people I do not know, observing the world around me in different ways, exploring what ignites my soul or what makes me sad have all revealed to me my path in life. This is not something that I have done in a few hours or even days. It has been done step by step. In another few years, my purpose may alter again or evolve and I should be open to this, too. At each stage of your life, the concept of success and fulfilment change, and your role as well. We all have different phases and different stages in life. How to be tapped in, tuned and aligned in each phase and stage that make the difference. For now, though, God has shown me my purpose in life, the reason I am here at this moment in time. Through prayer, meditation, self-exploration and listening to others, I have sought to inspire and educate. I believe the success of one of us should be the success of all. The achievement of one of us should be the driver for others to do more. The courage of one of us should open the door for many. Nowadays, my success is having a positive impact on people while having and maintaining my own peaceful life. Everyone has their own ideas of success: what ultimate success means to me may not be seen by others, as we all have different goals and motivations. I love how the American author Elizabeth Gilbert linked success with the feeling of "going home," by finding and pursuing something worthy that you love more than you love yourself. Every person you meet will recommend to you different recipes of success based on their own experiences or those of others they are connected to or inspired by. There is no right or wrong answer; what works for someone might not work for you. Nevertheless, what I have found is that there are three common ingredients: passion, positivity and perseverance, or as I like to call them: the "Magic 3Ps."

My thirty-fifth learning: We are all here for a higher purpose. We all have a why to pursue. Our purpose is best when it aligns with our true values as humans and is lived by every day.

Reflect and relate: What is your current definition of success?

Choose to lead with kindness, love and compassion.

_____

_____

_____

_____

_____

_____

_____

_____

_____

_____

_____

_____

Stepping Stone Thirty-Six: Be Kind, Rana

"Every good deed is charity."

—*Prophet Mohammad (Peace be upon him)*

Story thirty-six: Kindness was the key to unlocking my soul, and now I make it part of my everyday routine. Think about it: with all the other obstacles and barriers we have around us, to be unkind to ourselves and others is not helpful. It is actually cruelty. It is a disconnection with God and therefore disconnection with our true selves and the world around us. Kindness is a universal language that anyone can understand; it is what unites us on this earth. Kindness is just felt, and no prequalification is required. Being kind is treating others like you treat yourself. Therefore, rarely you can find people who are kind to others, but unkind to themselves. It is not about being right or wrong. It is not about being jealous or competitive; it is not about pointing out differences or judging people. Instead, kindness is about giving without expecting anything in return. Without the need of anything in return, the only reward is from God. When we support each other through kindness aren't we stronger together? I have found so much peace and tranquillity and joy in kindness, but I could not have found this had I not resolved first to be kind to myself. As I am developing and changing every day, I am also realising that as humans we all want the same. No matter where we are in life, how rich we are, where we live, which nationality, religion, race, sex or age we are, we all want to be treated with respect. But sometimes, we do not put kindness at the top of our priorities. We have the presumption that kindness equals weakness. On the contrary, kindness is strength. It took me years to figure that out. But what is real kindness? As I say, kindness is not giving to receiving nor it is just being kind without control or thought. I mentioned the continuous challenge that I face: being able to balance my needs between the needs of those that I love and care about. It is really difficult to think about yourself first when you are the hope-spreader, the universal-love believer and have a pure heart towards everyone. I get so much satisfaction from helping others and seeing them happy, and now, I have learned how to balance kindness towards myself with kindness towards other people. I am in control of my kindness, and therefore I am giving it now freely, generously and purely because it comes from the full cup. Kindness is also not about pushing people to do kind things just because we do. Everyone is on their own journey, and if others are not ready to let kindness in we should understand where they are on their path.

Practicing self-respect and kindness flow to others like a waterfall, clean, unforced and strong. I make it my mission to help others in any form I can. Practice every day small acts of kindness. How many of us compliment one another? How many of us highlight the good things in one another? Praying for others as well is one of the purest form of help, and it is for free. Think about how it feels to receive kind words, prayers and deeds. Doesn't a warm glow permeate through your whole being? Feel that. Share it and spread it. Make it your daily habit to give a compliment. Give that woman in the elevator with the great manicure a compliment, or the man with a great new haircut. Tell the mother who is dropping her kids to school that she is a super person by managing it all. Send that thank-you card to your colleague. Tell your friend how proud you are of him or her. Be kind to your new boss and embrace their good qualities. Open your heart to a person who is different than you, send prayers to your loved ones, and lastly, look at yourself in the mirror and tell yourself kindly: "I love your soul!" and mean it 100%.

My thirty-sixth learning: Kindness is in every one of us. We are all born to be kind, yet people misinterpret kindness as being weak. The most courageous people are the kindest. Kindness is a choice you will never regret.

Reflect and relate: Write down some "acts of kindness" you practice daily.

> Value kindness, peace, service, humility and love.

_____

_____

_____

_____

_____

_____

_____

_____

_____

_____

_____

_____

Stepping Stone Thirty-Seven: Between Trust and Hope, Magic Finds Its Way Back Home

"Believe in your heart that you're meant to live a life full of passion, purpose, magic and miracles."

—Roy T. Bennett, Author

Story thirty-seven: We all know the story of the genie, the magical lamp and the three wishes. Why limit magic to three wishes when we are limitless. We are the masters of our own lives and it is between trust and hope that magic finds its way back home. I call these the "aha" moments in life: the moments when we trust in God 100% and have 100% hope in the future. It is between surrendering to Him and living in the moment that magic is found. The excitement and suspense of life is magical in itself. Once we stop trying to control life and other people, we find that we can move towards our dreams effortlessly. Magic is the passion in our hearts, the glitter in our eyes and the hope in our souls. But magic needs to be nurtured. When our circumstances are not happy, as mine have been in the past, or life becomes too much we can turn our backs on magic. We can convince ourselves that believing is only for children, or that magic is silly or childish. I chose to keep believing. It is a cliché, but I know for sure that tomorrow will be a better day. The way I do this is by making a conscious effort every single day to increase my happiness through doing more of the things I love and keep believing because I know that the universe salutes the dreamers, the changers, the revolvers, the ones who are not scared to show their uniqueness, the authentic ones, the high vibrational ones, the ones who dare, the ones who follow their souls, the ones who lead by their hearts because this is their truth and the universe admires the believers. To live life more fully and make each day count, my magic moments are all about taking new chances and opportunities. It is about saying "yes" to life, instead of "no." It is my bank account that I keep topping up every day. I am responsible for my happiness account, and I have to fill it with moments that bring magic back into my life and keep that account in credit and not debit.

This had opened up my senses. I am now open to experiencing the best of everything. Nothing is too good for me, and nothing is too good to be true. Life loves me and there is a lavish and abundant limitless universe inside of me. There is more than enough good to go around, so many opportunities for good, so much kindness, resources, ideas, talent, understanding, inspiration, support and great connections. There is no limitation or ceiling to what I can be, do or experience. I am lining up with my greater good as I give thanks for all that has already been given and received. I am happy in my own and joyfully open to even more good.

I believe we all need magic to thrive. If we reject it, we reject a huge part of ourselves and our potential in life, and this creates anxiety and stress. Once we open our eyes, we understand magic is waiting for us around every corner – with flying unicorns.

My thirty-seventh learning: You are the creator of your own magical moments. Magic is found in trust and hope and having the adventurous spirit to indulge more in life.

Reflect and relate: Remind yourself with five magical moments that you have experienced in your life.

> "When two givers indulge in a connection, it is like magic. It is alchemy.
> I water you, you water me.
> We never drain each other, we just grow" – Unkown

_____

_____

_____

_____

_____

_____

_____

_____

_____

Stepping Stone Thirty-Eight: We Are All Connected, We All Matter

> *"Spend 5 minutes at the beginning of each day remembering we all want the same things (to be happy and be loved) and we are all connected to one another."*

—*Dalai Lama, Spiritual Leader*

Story thirty-eight: In the darkest moments of my life, described in the first chapters of this book, I did not believe in the power of connection. I struggled to understand other people outside of the dark hole I put myself in. I battled with my connection to God. It is amazing how darkness traps us in a world of negativity and pain – if only we could see what is on the other side! I have spoken at length about how I regained my connection to God, and how my faith has been restored and completed with certainty. In reaching a connection with him, I began reaching connection with others. The first time I really felt this was when I travelled to Mykonos, Greece, as part of my year of self-exploration. There, I was lucky enough to meet great people at a retreat and started great friendships with some. I realised that regardless of where we are from and what we do in life, we are all the same: connection is fostered through our differences as much as our resemblances. It was the power of togetherness pushing me forward that I remember the most. I would have never finished that hike, yoga class, those sit-ups and push-ups without the support of people around me. I would not have enjoyed my time as much as I did without the laughs, conversations, comments, inspiration, support, kindness and love of the team I met. I would have never survived the mosquito bites, the motion sickness and the fear of heights if people were not around me encouraging me at those times. The same experience of connection, when I summited Mount Kilimanjaro, the highest mountain in Africa. I would have not done it without the courageous and kindest mountain guides that accompanied us.

I shared the same connection experience recently when I was in quarantine. I used the time productively to connect with people and help each other to get through toughest times. We supported each other, checked on each other, laughed, sang and danced together in spirit while we were quarantined, passed on our good vibes and energy and lifted each other's spirits. Having to wear a mask and gloves and protective clothing to connect with the outside world and for as basic issues as receiving food was not a pleasant experience, yet I knew that I was not alone. It was interesting to me that at a time when we were required to socially distance from people physically, those were the times when we as humans got more connected. Those were the times that I have never felt more than ever that we are in this universe together as humans. Being open to the connection we have with other people has other positive effects too, effects that reverberate around the world. Instead of mistrusting others, we move towards a place of acceptance. After all, we are all created by Him. We all wake up every morning and experience the same feelings: love, joy and pleasure, sadness, despair, fear and loss. These are the very human emotions that keep us all connected. We are all beautiful emotional human beings after all. If we take a collective approach, we realise that we are part of a much bigger scheme of life, and every action of one person can affect the other.

My thirty-eighth learning: We are so powerful together. Alone, we can only be half as powerful. By joining forces, we can change the world to make it a better place.

Reflect and relate: How do you foster your connection to the world?

"We are the world
We are the children
We are the ones who make a brighter day, so let's tart giving
Oh, there is a choice we are making
We are saving our own lives
It is true we'll make a better day, just you and me."
— We Are the World song by USA for Africa.

Stepping Stone Thirty-Nine: I Found My True Voice: Now at Forty

"I now see how owning our story and loving ourselves through that process is the bravest thing that we will ever do."

—*Brené Brown, Researcher, Author and Storyteller*

Story thirty-nine: I have found now my most truthful voice – it has only taken me forty years! And, I am still learning to be more authentic and true to myself every day. As a woman, I think it is particularly important to learn to express ourselves and find our own styles, personalities and experiences in ways that are true to us. Many years ago, before I started on this journey towards the light, I would not have considered telling people my story. I was broken and ashamed. I wanted to hide my experiences from the world. I thought that if I communicated my story to others then no one would understand. Yet the complete opposite has been true. Through my journey, I have discovered that other people have felt at certain points in life the same despair I had and the only way we can connect with ourselves and others is by sharing our stories. When we find our true voices, we embrace our imperfections. We say: "What I have been through is part of me. I own my story now and my own voice."

In the deepest moments of despair, I found myself. Somewhere between reality and fantasy, I found a place that I can be me. A place above the skies, between the stars and beyond imagination. A place where I escape from my physical being, physical needs and physical attraction and rise above and deeper. I came to a realisation that resisting life closes all doors. Hence, I decided to surrender. I surrender to the universe with all its majestic moments. I accept and flow with the concept of Oneness. That I am the spirit and flesh of a beautiful creation that is here to do something, to be something and live everything. I have always been blessed and protected, but now I see my life as flowing as I want it to be because I have controlled the demons in me. For the first time since a while, my voice is only one of love, compassion and understanding. My space is less crowded with people, events and time to fulfil any temporary need, instead I am choosing to live in depth and let my being and heart guide me. For me, that is more important than anything, and loving God underpins all of who I am. Of course, there are times when I am afraid to use my voice, afraid to speak my opinion. But I forced myself to. As long as I know my intentions are good I face my fears each and every day. Fear no longer chained me around. It actually has chosen to set me free when it realised that even its mighty force could not stop me from creating life. My journey towards the light has, most of all, been told in the peace I have found within. I am at my best when all the parts of me are fully aligned. When my mind, heart, body and soul all work in harmony there I find my perfect melodies and dance with life every day. Finally, at forty years of age, I know how to bring those parts together and harmonise them, and find peace within especially at times of distress. My voice may not be pleasant to everyone, but true beauty is the acceptance that there are many different voices that make up this world, each as important as the other and each is valuable.

My thirty-ninth learning: Embrace your own voice before you become a voice for others. Speak up even if you are shaking inside. If you have not found your true voice yet, search for it, understand it. Through it, you will understand who you are.

Reflect and relate: What is your true calling?

Look back at your life and celebrate it.
You are here for a reason and you matter.

Stepping Stone Forty: The Courage to Be Who I Am

"For what it's worth: it's never too late or, in my case, too early to be whoever you want to be. There's no time limit, stop whenever you want. You can change or stay the same, there are no rules to this thing. We can make the best or the worst of it. I hope you make the best of it. And I hope you see things that startle you. I hope you feel things you never felt before. I hope you meet people with a different point of view. I hope you live a life you're proud of. If you find that you're not, I hope you have the courage to start all over again."

—Eric Roth, Screenwriter

Story forty: When I started this book, it was difficult for me to look back on my life and see that, at times, I had lost my way. I found some of it painful and emotional; I cried and laughed. What I realised most of all is that my past has not defined who I am today. I have come out from that place, stronger, happier and more humble, and to do that I have needed courage. I have needed love within me. Courage is a key ingredient in facing all of life's demons. Courage is not about being flawless and stern all the time. It is about entering the world with the curiosity of a child, the curiosity of the little girl I have described throughout this book. But it is also about being wise and learning the power of choice, tempered with a love for ourselves. Instead of surrounding ourselves with negative energy, we draw in positive vibrations and emit these to the world, like watching a kaleidoscope of butterflies flap their wings on the air. Although fear sometimes crops up into my life uninvited, unleashed and untamed like a swirl of perplexing emotion. I confirmed that it is essential for survival and a catalyst for growth.

It is a motivator to take one step further into the journey of life. One step at a time and one act of bravery is what is needed every day. Even when fear chooses us as its shelter, we refuse to let it in and stay for a longer time within our warm beings and instead choose to face it ahead with courage. I choose now to stand tall looking fear in the eyes unbothered because I am now learning the power of choice. The power of choosing myself. I hope that reading this book has given you room to explore and know who you are and who do you want to be. I hope it gives you the opportunity to discover your own voice and own courageous authentic self by discovering mine. Wherever you are in life, or whatever journey you are on, we can all move forward across the stepping stones of life. Sometimes we will step back on our journey, and those stepping back moves are there for a reason and part of the journey. With practice, perseverance, compassion and faith we know, eventually, we will be headed in the right direction. Courage is about freeing ourselves of the fear that keeps us trapped in one place, scared to open up our hearts and souls to love to run through our veins, and make the best out of our lives. In the end we all get what we value most. If we do not like what we have, look at what we value. Our world will blossom when we choose love over separation and fear. From the moment I made a decision on my mission to live fearlessly, I gained so much courage. I left miserable relationships behind. I excelled at my job. Despite our physical separation, I formed a deep and loving relationship with my sons. I have grown as a human being. Now I am opening myself to all life's blessings with curiosity, love and passion. And I am making a beautiful connection with people and the universe, looking forward for a new love to sweep my being with its mighty force. Most of all, I have found the courage to live the present, manifest and face the future. The journey of life is continuous and flowing. I might change directions as I am work in progress, but I am open to experience the best of everything.

Daily peace and endless abundance come from choosing Oneness, and forgiveness. Remember that ego judges, fears, separates, and attaches, and that people will always remember how you made them feel. There is a new circle of life emerging now, but this time it is as the sun in its size, warmth, depth, light, wholeness, brightness, deliberate intention of glowing, growing and spreading light across.

What do I want to leave behind? What do I want to leave as a legacy? I could answer this persisting question now:

My Journey of Life – My Journey Towards Courage And Within My Heart Is My Legacy.

My fortieth learning: Never apologise for being who you are. You are the embodiment of your life's story: your struggles and pain and your successes and achievements. Treat every day as an opportunity to learn and evolve further through life. Live each day with love, kindness, courage and passion. Safeguard and keep nurturing the inner connection.

Reflect and relate: Reflect on your own journey of life. It is your unique journey towards love, light and courage. Design, construct and experience every step of it.

_____

_____

_____

_____

_____

_____

_____

_____

_____

_____

_____

_____

_____

LAST PAGE

"I learned that courage was not the absence of fear, but the triumph over it. The brave man is not he who does not feel afraid, but he who conquers that fear."

— *Nelson Mandela, Political Leader and Philanthropist*

A LOVE LETTER FROM ME TO YOU

Ask yourself how you really are, and who you are for real.

Trust that your unquestioning belief will always guide you.

Never be ashamed of your feelings. They are your inner guides.

Never be afraid of standing out, or standing apart, just because you choose to think, live and be different.

Live by no one else's standards but your own truth.

See with your heart and love with your soul.

Never let the echoes of fear or loneliness hold you back from loving.

Shower everyone with love and positivity and the sunshine of your smile.

Trust in Him, and in your faith. It will guide you through.

Just because you are here, choose to be joyful and kind, no matter how you feel and see how it nourishes your soul and others.

Be giving like a beautiful tree that shelters everyone with its unconditional love, but do not lose yourself in the process.

Give with no expectations and expect the best because that is what you deserve and that is who you are.

Nourish your body, heart, mind and soul with nurturing food, emotions, ideas and connections, and constantly water those from the river of life: only let pure, transparent and flowing energy in.

Hug the sunbeams of your soul and know how loved you are every single day.

Just be the way you are right now.

Because you are enough as you are.

May faith guide you, fear test you, love lift you and light show you the way forward.

May you find the courage to accept every step of your journey as it unfolds and surrender to the beauty of the unknowns.

May you thrive in life to be kind and let the world witness your humanity before your cruelty.

May you find courage in every step of your journey.

May you find courage to speak from your heart.

May you live fearlessly.

May you answer the question: "But REALLY, How Are You?" now courageously, truthfully and with love.

I love and honour each one of you.

Rana x